"Portia Collins's first encounter with the gospel in the book of Galatians proved to be a watershed experience for her, as it has been for countless others. It led her into a life of freedom, hope, and joy she had never known was possible. Now she guides you on a journey through this small but mighty epistle, desiring that you, too, will discover the transforming, amazing grace of Christ in a fresh way."
Nancy DeMoss Wolgemuth, Founder and Bible Teacher, Revive Our Hearts

"When I think of Portia Collins, I think of one of the biggest cheerleaders I know for encouraging women to study and encounter the truths of the gospel for themselves. In this Bible study on Galatians, she does just that. Helping you with foundational Bible study skills as well as showing you how to discover truths that will transform your life, Portia is a trusted guide to take you deeper into Scripture and to help you fall in love with God's word."
Laura Wifler, coauthor, *Risen Motherhood* and *Gospel Mom*

"*Finding Freedom in Christ* is a helpful and enriching guide through Paul's letter to the Galatians, revealing the life-changing truths of the gospel. With wisdom and clarity, Portia Collins encourages readers to apply these truths to their daily lives and embrace the freedom Christ offers. This Bible study is an excellent resource for any woman longing to grow in her faith and walk freely in the grace of God."
Melissa Kruger, author; Vice President of Discipleship Programming, The Gospel Coalition

"This resource is a treasure. Whether for new believers, seasoned Christians, or Bible study groups, it provides both conviction and encouragement—just as Galatians itself does. Portia skillfully unpacks the setting and context of Paul's letter while guiding readers to engage deeply with the text. Rather than spoon-feeding answers, she asks insightful questions that sharpen our exegetical skills and, ultimately, deepen our love for the Lord Jesus Christ."
Quina Aragon, author, *Love Has a Story*

"I am excited to recommend *Finding Freedom in Christ* to women of all ages! Portia Collins helps us study Galatians through faithful observation, interpretation, and application. Whether you are new to the faith or a seasoned believer, this is a resource that will encourage you to live in the freedom Christ offers, rooted in the grace he provides."
Hunter Beless, author; Founder, Journeywomen Ministries

"This is a rich, wide-reaching, exegetical look at Galatians wrapped in Portia's inviting and relatable teaching style. Full of charts, definitions, cross-references, little-known facts, and opportunities for personal reflection, this book will help women walk away with a more thorough understanding of Scripture. *Finding Freedom in Christ* models Bible study best practices for women who are serious about learning how to dig into God's word to come out changed."
Emily A. Jensen, coauthor, *Risen Motherhood* and *Gospel Mom*

Finding Freedom in Christ

Finding Freedom in Christ

An 8-Week Study of Galatians

PORTIA COLLINS

WHEATON, ILLINOIS

Finding Freedom in Christ: An 8-Week Study of Galatians

© 2025 by Portia Collins

Published by Crossway
    1300 Crescent Street
    Wheaton, Illinois 60187

All rights reserved. No part of this publication may be reproduced, stored in a retrieval system, or transmitted in any form by any means, electronic, mechanical, photocopy, recording, or otherwise, without the prior permission of the publisher, except as provided for by USA copyright law. Crossway® is a registered trademark in the United States of America.

The timeline and maps found in this book are taken from the ESV® Study Bible (The Holy Bible, English Standard Version®), © 2008 by Crossway, a publishing ministry of Good News Publishers. Used by permission. All rights reserved.

Cover design and illustration: Crystal Courtney

First printing 2025

Printed in China

Unless otherwise indicated, Scripture quotations are from the ESV® Bible (The Holy Bible, English Standard Version®), © 2001 by Crossway, a publishing ministry of Good News Publishers. Used by permission. All rights reserved. The ESV text may not be quoted in any publication made available to the public by a Creative Commons license. The ESV may not be translated in whole or in part into any other language.

Scripture quotations marked CSB have been taken from the Christian Standard Bible®, copyright © 2017 by Holman Bible Publishers. Used by permission. Christian Standard Bible® and CSB® are federally registered trademarks of Holman Bible Publishers.

Scripture quotations marked NLT are taken from the Holy Bible, New Living Translation, copyright © 1996, 2004, 2015 by Tyndale House Foundation. Used by permission of Tyndale House Publishers, a Division of Tyndale House Ministries, Carol Stream, Illinois 60188. All rights reserved.

Trade paperback ISBN: 978-1-4335-9483-0
ePub ISBN: 978-1-4335-9485-4
PDF ISBN: 978-1-4335-9484-7

Crossway is a publishing ministry of Good News Publishers.

RRD		34	33	32	31	30	29	28	27	26	25
15	14	13	12	11	10	9	8	7	6	5	4	3	2	1

Contents

Introduction: Becoming a Good Exegete *1*

Week 1   Embracing the True Gospel of Freedom (Galatians 1:1–24) *7*

Week 2   Standing Firm in Freedom (Galatians 2:1–21) *31*

Week 3   The Promise of Freedom (Galatians 3:1–14) *53*

Week 4   The Pathway to Freedom (Galatians 3:15–24) *71*

Week 5   The Identity of Freedom (Galatians 3:25–29) *93*

Week 6   Heirs of Freedom (Galatians 4:1–31) *113*

Week 7   Freedom in the Spirit (Galatians 5:1–26) *135*

Week 8   Living Free in Christ (Galatians 6:1–18) *155*

Galatians Wrap-Up *175*

Appendix: Praying Through Galatians *179*

Notes *183*

Introduction

BECOMING A GOOD EXEGETE

VIDEO 1

As a vibrant twentysomething-year-old, I was on a difficult quest to find my true identity. Every aspect of my life seemed hard during that season. Yet these struggles had a wonderful side effect—they caused my desire for God's word to greatly increase. One evening in particular, I planted myself on the floor of my small two-bedroom apartment and began reading the beautiful book of Galatians. As I sat there in the quiet, reading page after page, I began to weep. The message of salvation by grace through faith in Jesus Christ that is recorded in Galatians pierced through the noise of my life and spoke directly to my weary and anxious heart. My life had swung between the two poles of legalism and lawlessness. Sometimes I thought that my religious rule-keeping was enough to earn me righteousness before God. But then I would go in the completely opposite direction by indulging in sin under the guise of freedom. It was a vicious cycle that left me confused, lost, and constantly searching for hope in all the wrong places.

Thankfully, God, in his infinite mercy and grace, gave me true hope through the truth of his word. As I studied Galatians, I was confronted with the reality of my own proclivity toward the two extremes of legalism and lawlessness. The Scriptures acted like a mirror that revealed the futility of trying to justify myself through my own means, and for the first time—even though I had grown up in the church—I clearly understood the gospel.

Opening my Bible to Galatians that night changed my life in the most magnificent ways. The teachings of Galatians gave me a comforting reminder that a life bound by legalistic practices could not bring me any closer to God, and a life marred by lawlessness could not keep me from truly receiving the grace and freedom that God offers to his beloved children. Through faith in

Jesus Christ, I found the true freedom that my soul longed for after so many years. Now, year after year, I experience the joy of repeatedly mining the words of Paul to gain a deeper understanding of this truth.

As I reflect on that evening when I first read the book of Galatians, I now see how this seemingly simple act of reading the Scriptures led me to a new life in Christ. God's word was the catalyst that set me free. Needless to say, I am so grateful to the Lord for guiding me into a rich understanding of what it really means to be saved by grace through faith and to be free in Christ Jesus. This, my friend, is a precious gift that continues to shape my walk with God every day, and I hope that through studying Galatians with me, you will experience the same.

The Best Way to Study God's Word

"That's a nice story," you may say, "but how exactly am I supposed to study the Bible?" That is what I'm here to help with. In short, the best way to study Scripture is by using exegesis. "Exe-what?" you say. Don't worry; that's what I said too. When I first heard the word *exegesis*, I didn't know how to pronounce it or what it meant. I was sifting through online resources about studying the Bible while sitting at my desk when the word caught my eye. Although I stumbled through its pronunciation more times than I'd like to admit (it's " ˌek-sə-ˈjē-səs"),[1] I was completely gripped by this fascinating concept. In short, exegeting the Bible means interpreting it by drawing meaning from the text. People who practice exegesis are called "exegetes." Initially, I thought that title was reserved for pastors or reverends, not for ordinary people like me and you. But approaching the Bible in this methodical way is not only something that regular people *can* do; it's actually something that we *must* do. Only by properly exegeting Scripture can we truly understand what it says and apply its life-giving power to our hearts. Through this study, I hope to train you to become a good exegete—someone who draws accurate and meaningful conclusions about the Bible by simply following the text and applying ordinary reading principles.

Think of it this way: When we read a letter, we never start in the middle of a sentence or the middle of the letter. We read beginning to end, starting with the first word of the first sentence and ending with the last. We read the letter page by page, seeking to understand the full context of what the writer is communicating. Reading the Bible is no different. While this is a special collection of books containing the very words of God, the Bible is still a literary work and should be read as such. It is not a collection of disjointed, random stories, but one big story that reveals who God is and what his redemptive plan is for humanity. To understand the fullness of God's redemptive plan (as much as is humanly possible), we must be diligent students of Scripture. We must read line by line, making note of words, phrases, people, and places. Ideally, we engage the text inductively by asking thoughtful questions that lead us to God's intended meaning instead of forcing our own preconceived ideas on the text to make it say what we want it to say.

Overall, exegeting the Bible well as believers today is marked by three steps: reading, examining, and applying. Let's look at each now.

Reading

First, and most obviously, we must read a passage in order to exegete it. And there's a lot that we can learn about God by reading the Bible over and over again and with intention! Our brains often start to make sense of the literary or historical context of a passage (the importance of which I explain below) by identifying key people, places, and other details when we read and reread. It is only by reading the Bible on a daily basis over many years that God's message for us starts to sink into our souls. But take heart—though it requires hard work to set aside time for reading God's word, it pays off in dividends to our souls, our relationships, our work, and every other area of life.

Examining

Yet simply reading the Bible is not enough. Though God gives us all we need for life and godliness in the Bible (2 Pet. 1:3), and though anyone can understand its basic message without theological training, the fact is that the Bible was written years ago by people in a completely different context from ours. Thus, examining the historical and literary context of a passage is crucial for truly understanding it. These pieces of contextual information clarify the author's intent, which helps us get to what he was really saying to his audience in his own time and what God is really saying to us today.

In order to get at this contextual information, we need to ask questions about the author, audience, place, purpose, genre, and canonical location of the text. Who wrote it? To whom, where, and why? Is the text law, history, wisdom, poetry, narrative, a parable, or a letter? What verses, chapters, and books surround it? We must also examine the text itself—the structure of the sentences, the definition of terms, and the functions of the various parts of speech. Further, we must pay attention to words and phrases that are repeated, because repetition in the Bible is much like the bold-faced and italicized words in our modern texts—it is meant to draw our attention to something important. Understanding these elements helps us discern God's intended meaning of the text. Remember, Scripture always means what God intended it to mean.

To figure all of this out, it can help to use a study Bible. The *ESV Study Bible* is among my favorites. If you want to enhance your studies even more, consider investing in a concordance, lexicon, Bible dictionary, Bible encyclopedia, or commentary. These are all resources you can use to help you examine the Scriptures. You'll also find QR codes for videos with additional instruction about Galatians at various places throughout this study guide to help you answer the questions.

Applying

After we examine Scripture, we can properly apply it to our lives in practical ways. And by asking questions about personal and communal application, we bridge the gap between understanding the text and living it out. Application is where Scripture shifts from being theoretical to becoming a reality in our daily lives.

As imperfect beings, we're capable of misinterpreting and misapplying the Scriptures. But if we dig deeper into God's word through exegesis, we can listen and truly understand not only what God was saying to the original audience but also what he is saying to us today. The Scriptures are used by the Holy Spirit to teach, rebuke, correct, and train us in righteousness so that we might be fully equipped for every good work (2 Tim. 3:16–17). The Spirit speaks through the Scripture to teach us what is true, and it is impossible to understand God without the Spirit's work. Thus, God's nature, ways, and plan are sufficiently revealed through the Scriptures and rightly applied to our lives through the work of the Holy Spirit. The two work hand in hand.

Studying God's Word Together

Though some aspects of studying the Bible are best done in quiet contemplation and prayer, it is also important to read, examine, and apply God's word with God's people. Thus, while this study of Galatians can certainly be completed on your own, I have designed it to be a combination of individual and group study so that after completing the individual study questions, you can gather with sisters in Christ to discuss what you learned using the group discussion questions included at the end of each week. There is a sweet blessing that God gives when we meet together. In my years of studying God's word, my most special and cherished moments happened among dear sisters in Christ. Friend, please don't miss that blessing.

If you have never studied the Bible by reading, examining, and applying, then I'll admit that you might feel a bit intimidated right now. This might be the point where you are questioning whether you want to commit or if you're even capable of seeing this study through to the end. The good news is that I have designed this study to guide you through the steps of exegesis and equip you with the skills needed to become a great exegete. At the end, you'll walk away with not just a deeper understanding of Galatians but also the confidence to study other books of the Bible more effectively.

Right now, I want to encourage you to reject all notions of self-doubt and negativity as you prepare to work through this study. May the words of our brother Paul raise your spirit:

> I do not cease to give thanks for you, remembering you in my prayers, that the God of our Lord Jesus Christ, the Father of glory, may give you the Spirit of wisdom and of revelation in the knowledge of him, having the eyes of your hearts enlightened, that you may know what is the hope to which he has called you, what are the riches of his glorious inheritance in the saints, and what is the immeasurable greatness of his power toward us who believe. (Eph. 1:16–19)

In the same spirit and mind as Paul, I am also praying for you. I am fully confident in the Lord's extraordinary ability to lead and guide you through his word with much wisdom and clarity. I invite you to embark on this journey in faith, trusting that God is near as we seek to understand the truth of his word by the power of the Holy Spirit.

Week 1

EMBRACING THE TRUE GOSPEL OF FREEDOM
(GALATIANS 1:1–24)

We go to Christ for forgiveness, and then too often
look to the law for the power to fight our sins.

C. H. SPURGEON

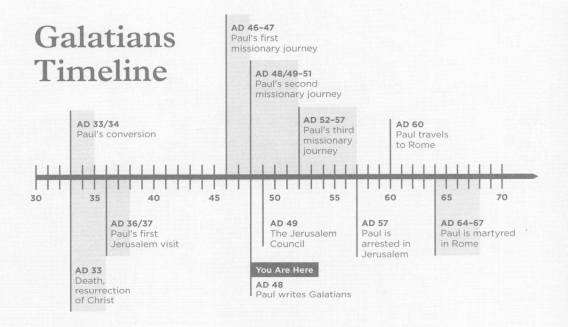

VIDEO 2

Welcome to our first week of studying Galatians! Aren't you excited? Grab your pens, highlighters, and—most importantly—your Bible, because we are ready to explore the depths of God's grace and faithfulness as recounted by the apostle Paul in this letter.

Grace is the overarching theme of this book and the cornerstone of Christian doctrine—people are saved by God's grace. For many non-Christians, the concept of grace can be a bit baffling. I'm not an expert in other religions, but I've learned a thing or two about what non-Christians believe about attaining salvation. Consider these examples:

- Buddhists believe that salvation is reached by following the path of enlightenment, which is found only through dedicated preparation, meditation, and ascetic living (i.e., abstaining from worldly pleasures to achieve spiritual goals).

Galatians 1:1–24

- Hindus believe that salvation is gained through spiritual liberation, which is brought about by a repeated cycle of birth, death, and rebirth.
- Muslims believe that salvation is achieved by doing good deeds and strictly adhering to certain prayer and fasting rituals.

You'd probably agree that these religions are pretty different from Christianity. However, some religious traditions that appear to have Christian origins also communicate a message very different from salvation by grace. Here are a few examples:

- Jehovah's Witnesses believe that salvation is achieved by performing works like door-to-door evangelism.
- Mormons, also known as members of the Church of Jesus Christ of Latter-day Saints, believe that salvation is granted not only by God's grace but also through the practice of Mormon temple rituals and unyielding faithfulness to Mormon church leaders.
- Black Hebrew Israelites believe that salvation is given to the true people of Israel—namely, people of African descent—when they strictly follow Old Testament laws and practices.

It's clear that all of these religions and religious cults share a common belief: that humans must attain to their own salvation. Whether through meditation, ethical living, strict adherence to laws or practices, or even being born with a specific ethnicity, the burden is always on a person to merit salvation rather than receiving the grace of God alone.

Thankfully, Christianity is different in that it proclaims that sinful human beings are saved by grace. That's it! Not our works, practices, or identity, but solely the grace of God. The fundamental belief of Christianity is that human effort, no matter how sincere or intense, is never enough to attain true freedom. Salvation is accomplished by Jesus Christ, and all who believe in him are recipients of God's good grace and freed from the chains of sin. Whew; talk about a hallelujah moment!

Galatians is a pointed letter that highlights how a "gospel" that simply tacks Jesus on at the end of a list of human requirements is essentially no gospel at all. The entire letter can be explained in this way: If faith in Jesus Christ must be supplemented with human deeds to ensure salvation, that's really bad news, but—praise God!—he gives us all we need for salvation in Christ.

Take some time to reflect on the implications of grace in your life. Have you ever been tempted to add something to the gospel (e.g., good works or an aspect of your identity)? This week, I hope that God's goodness and grace shine bright through your studies. I hope that you'll be reminded of how salvation offered through Jesus Christ is the pathway to true freedom and how living under grace ultimately leads us to a deeper, more fulfilling relationship with God and people. Let's get started!

WEEK 1 | DAY 1
Galatians 1:1–5

Read Galatians 1. After reading the entire chapter, focus on verses 1–5 and answer the following questions:

◘ Who is the author of this letter?

Key Terms

Apostle: a special messenger designated by Jesus Christ to proclaim his teachings to others

Judaizers: Jewish Christians who pressured non-Jewish believers to follow Jewish customs

Grace: unmerited favor from God (that cannot be earned)

Galatians 1:1–24

- Who are the recipients of this letter (i.e., to whom was it written)?

- How does the author describe himself in verse 1? Note the contrast that he makes. Specifically, how does this contrast undergird Paul's authority?

- Paul wrote thirteen of the books found in the New Testament, including Philippians. Take a moment to read Philippians 1:1–2. Compare how Paul describes himself in these verses with how he describes himself at the outset of Galatians. What is different about Paul's description of himself? What differences do you notice in tone?

- Why do you think Paul describes himself differently to these two audiences? (Reading both Galatians and Philippians in their entirety may help answer this question. Feel free to come back to this question later in the week.)

◘ In the first few verses of Galatians, Paul establishes a firm foundation on which he will build the rest of his case concerning faith, redemption, justification, adoption, restoration, freedom, and ultimately, the love of God. We must not miss exactly why Paul begins his letter in this way. In verse 1, Paul has already told us who he is, who sent him, and the mighty work of the one who sent him. In verse 2, Paul mentions "all the brothers who are with me." Paul's words here highlight a sense of unity. Read Romans 6:3–4. How do these verses help us to understand better what Paul is saying in Galatians 1:2?

◘ We see the first mention of the word "grace" in verse 3. Continue reading verses 3–5 and answer the following questions:

- According to Paul, who gives "grace and peace" to us?

- What did Jesus Christ do to attain grace and peace for those who believe?

- Where did the plan to attain grace and peace come from?

- How should we respond to the grace and peace given to us?

Personal Reflection

So far we are only five verses into our study, but Paul has already provided foundational information that will help us develop a biblical understanding of grace. How has this passage reaffirmed, challenged, or deepened your understanding of grace? Based on Paul's words here, what can we, as believers, conclude about our need for grace (vv. 3–4)?

WEEK 1 | DAY 2
Galatians 1:6–10

Reread Galatians 1. After rereading the entire chapter, focus on verses 6–10 and answer the following questions:

- At this point, Paul quickly transitions from his greeting and jumps right into the heart of what he wants to discuss. What is Paul's problem with the Galatian church?

- In verse 6, Paul uses the word "gospel," which means "good news" in Greek. Read Romans 5:1–11. How does this passage help you to understand that the gospel of Christ is good news?

Galatians 1:1–24

- In Galatians 1:7, Paul describes those who teach a different, or a false, gospel. According to Paul, what are the primary characteristics of a false teacher?

- Why is a different or distorted gospel no gospel at all?

- To underscore the seriousness of preaching another gospel, Paul offers some pretty stern words to the Galatians. What does Paul say of people and even angels who distort the one true gospel?

- The Greek word for "curse" is *anathema*, which is where the English word comes from. Look up this word in an English dictionary. How does its definition help you understand Paul's warning?

▢ In verse 10, Paul unpacks his motivations for writing such a stern rebuke, highlighting that his goal is not to win the approval of people. Ultimately, who does Paul aim to please?

The History of Galatia

Galatia was a unique city that now is part of modern Turkey (see fig. 1). Originally part of a Celtic region, Galatia became a Roman province (that is, a territory located outside of Rome but still under Roman control) in 25 BC. Galatia's Celtic roots and Roman governance created an interesting dynamic that transformed the city into a melting pot of diverse cultures, ethnicities, and religions. As shown in figure 2, Paul's first missionary journey brought him to many cities in southern Galatia. (You can read about this particular journey in Acts 13–14.) Though Galatia was an ideal location for sharing the gospel, establishing a church there came with serious challenges. For example, the Galatians faced conflicts regarding cultural differences between Jews and Gentiles. Specifically, the Judaizers—a group of Christian Jews who falsely taught that everyone of non-Jewish descent must be circumcised—threatened the gospel-centered ministry of Paul. This made confusion and conflict run rampant in the Galatian church. Fortunately, Paul did not consider the Galatian believers to be a lost cause. Thus, his letter to them is a passionate plea to reject the legalism and any cultural conformity that leads to abandoning the truth of the gospel. Most importantly, he wants them to keep their eyes fixed on Jesus. Paul's ultimate goal in writing to the Galatians was to provide a stern yet loving appeal to remember the true gospel that he first shared with them.[1]

Galatians 1:1–24

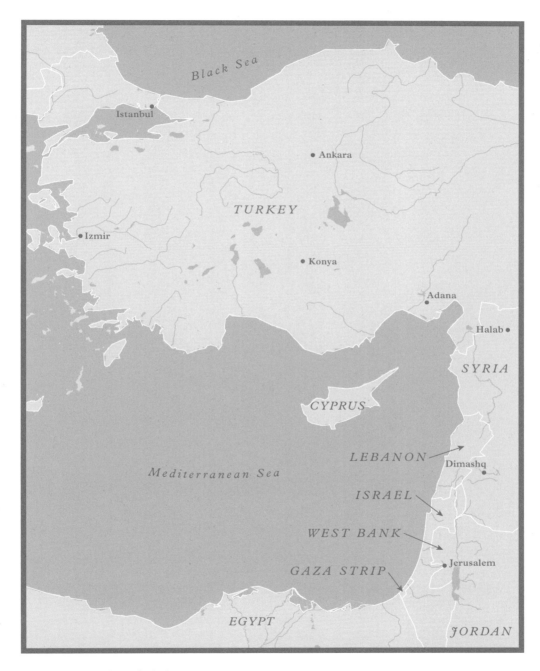

Figure 1. Modern Galatia

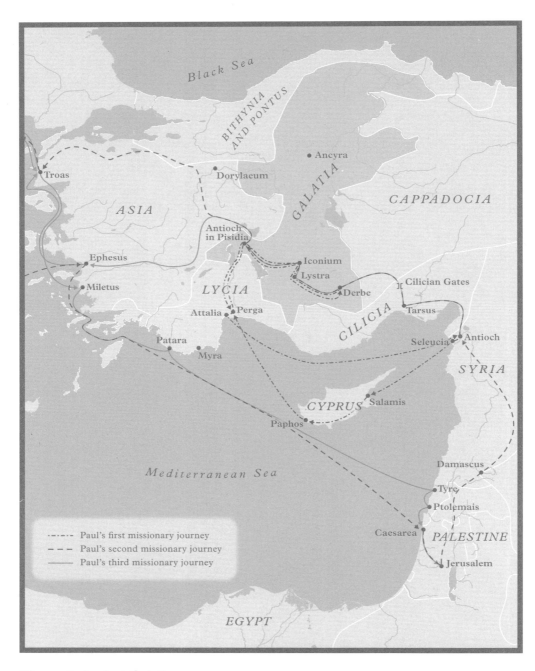

Figure 2. Ancient Galatia

Personal Reflection

Do you feel convicted by Paul's words in this passage? When it comes to sharing the gospel, have you ever fallen short by seeking to please man with your words more than you seek to please God (Gal. 1:10)? Take time to write out a confession to God. Ask God to help you live obediently and to eagerly share the gospel at every opportunity, just as Paul did.

WEEK 1 | DAY 3
Galatians 1:11–16a

Reread Galatians 1. After rereading the entire chapter, focus on verses 11–16a and answer the following questions:

- Paul begins this section by making a distinctive claim about the gospel that he preaches and elaborates on in the following verses. According to Paul, how is the gospel that he shares different from false gospels (vv. 11–12)?

- In verse 13, Paul mentions his former way of life. Take a moment to read Acts 8:1–9:2 and 26:4; Philippians 3:5–6; and Mark 7:3. How do these passages shed light on Paul's former way of life?

Galatians 1:1–24

- Paul also describes himself formerly as "advancing in Judaism" and "extremely zealous" for the traditions of his ancestors (v. 14). What does this say about Paul's preconversion motivations?

- In verse 15, Paul recounts a pivotal point in his life. What caused such an abrupt and radical change?

- Read Isaiah 49:1, Jeremiah 1:5, and Romans 8:28–29. What do these passages teach us about being "set apart" and "called" by God (Gal. 1:15)?

- In your own words, explain the four ways that Paul emphasizes God's work in his life (vv. 15–16).

◻ Take a look at verse 15 and the beginning of verse 16. How does Paul describe the gift of grace that he received? Specifically pay attention to who is revealed to Paul and who makes the revelation to Paul (see Acts 9:3–19).

Personal Reflection

By highlighting his radical conversion, Paul supports the claim that the gospel he preaches is from God and is not his own or any other man's. Take a moment to reflect on God's grace in your own life. How did God open your eyes to the gospel? In what ways has Jesus Christ made himself known to you? What is God's call on your life?

WEEK 1 | DAY 4
Galatians 1:16b–20

Reread Galatians 1. After rereading the entire chapter, focus on verses 16b–20 and answer the following questions:

- Paul notes that immediately after his conversion, he did not "consult" with anyone regarding the gospel he received (v. 16b). Why did Paul not need to consult anyone?

- To further support this point, Paul notes that he also did not immediately go up to Jerusalem to confirm his apostolic calling. According to the text, where did Paul go?

- Read Acts 9:19–22. What was Paul doing in Damascus?

- According to Galatians 1:18, how many years passed before Paul actually arrived in Jerusalem after his conversion?

Did You Know?

Growing up, I really wanted to become an attorney. I fiercely pursued this career path until my junior year of college. I took courses to prime myself for law school, and I also joined high school and collegiate mock trial teams. As a result, I became relatively well-versed in what is commonly understood as the "rules of evidence." When an item of evidence is presented in a court of law, it must be authenticated in order to be admitted. However, some items of evidence are self-authenticating, which means they require no extrinsic evidence of authenticity. Examples of self-authenticating items of evidence are domestic or foreign documents that are signed and sealed by verified governmental personnel. The gospel of Jesus Christ is much like a self-authenticating piece of evidence. It does not require any extrinsic evidence to be received. This is why Paul did not need to confirm the gospel that he received with anyone else.

Galatians 1:1–24

- Who did Paul meet in Jerusalem?

- According to verse 18, the purpose of Paul's travel to Jerusalem was to "visit" Cephas (some translations, like the New Living Translation [NLT] and the Christian Standard Bible [CSB], phrase this as "get to know" or "become acquainted"). How does Paul's wording highlight the main reason for this visit? What does Paul's language suggest about what he was *not* coming to Jerusalem to do?

- In verse 20, Paul makes a solemn declaration before God, similar to how witnesses affirm the truth when taking the stand in a courtroom. What is Paul affirming, and why is it important for his message?

- Why do you think Paul chooses his words with such care and meticulously chronicles his travels after his conversion? What is he ultimately making a case for? (Hint: See Gal. 1:11–12.)

Personal Reflection

Take a moment to think about how wonderful it is to believe in the one true gospel that does not need the confirmation of any man. When we truly receive the gospel of Jesus Christ, we can confidently share that good news without fear or uncertainty. How does knowing this fuel your desire to evangelize the lost today?

WEEK 1 | DAY 5
Galatians 1:21–24

Reread Galatians 1. After rereading the entire chapter, focus on verses 21–24 and answer the following questions:

◘ Paul now draws our attention to another one of his postconversion travels. Let's take a moment to read and connect several passages in order to clearly understand this:

- Read Acts 22:3. Here we see that Paul is from Tarsus, the capital of Cilicia. According to Galatians 1:21, Paul's first missionary journey took him back to his home region. Let's put on our imaginative thinking caps: What might have been some reasons for Paul returning to his home region? What potential challenges or downsides could he have faced?

- Read Acts 22:17–21. What happened here? Who sent Paul to Cilicia and Syria? What does this reveal about who is ultimately behind all true ministry endeavors?

- Peter and several other apostles were ministering to Jews in Jerusalem. With whom was Paul called to share the gospel?

- Paul notes that while he was away on his travels, he remained "unknown" to the churches of Judea (v. 22). According to verse 23, what did those in Judea hear about Paul while he was away?

- What did the churches in Judea do in response to hearing about Paul (v. 24)?

Personal Reflection

As we close this first chapter of Galatians, it's vital to understand Paul's primary goal of explaining his conversion, postconversion travels, and relationship with other believers throughout Judea during the onset of his ministry. Though Paul makes the distinction that he received the gospel independent of the Jerusalem church, he also clarifies that he and the Jerusalem church shared the same gospel—the true gospel of Jesus Christ. Paul tells the Galatians that there is no other gospel and that it is the Judaizers who have departed from the truth, not him. He also notes that the Jerusalem church and the apostles rejoiced at hearing about God's work in his life. Would this be so if Paul had been teaching a false gospel? Absolutely not!

The gospel received by the revelation of Jesus Christ is not man's invention, and thus no human has the authority to change it. The gospel that Paul received and that we have received is the message of Jesus Christ. And when we receive the gospel of Jesus Christ, we are truly set free from the bondage of Satan and the systems of man. How does realizing this truth give you the confidence to reject and stand firm against false gospels that attempt to add to or take away from the complete and sufficient work of Christ?

Week 1 Group Discussion

1. What foundational truth lies at the heart of the gospel, and why is it considered good news for all who believe? Discuss with your group how the message of the gospel is transformational, and specifically how it has changed your life.

2. How is legalism different from the gospel? What might we be tempted to add to the gospel in our cultural context today? How does adding to the gospel in any way distort it, and how can we guard against doing that?

3. In Galatians 1:8–9, Paul issues a stern warning against altering the gospel, saying that those who distort the gospel are cursed. Why is Paul's language so severe? What happens when the gospel is altered?

4. Consider what it means to contend or fight for the gospel. Is this something that you do regularly? In what ways? Why is it critical that we are always ready to make a defense for the hope that is in us (1 Pet. 3:15)?

5. How does your understanding of the gospel shape your actions and interactions with others? Practically speaking, how does knowing the gospel help you better engage with both believers and nonbelievers?

6. Think of those in your life who have rejected the gospel or perhaps believe a false gospel. How do Paul's encounter with Christ and his subsequent conversion provide hope for witnessing to the lost people in your life? How can you find encouragement as you continue to hope for their salvation?

7. What did you learn about the nature of grace from studying Paul's conversion this week? How have your own tendencies toward works-righteousness been challenged through this week's studies?

Week 2

STANDING FIRM IN FREEDOM

(GALATIANS 2:1–21)

This is the true meaning of Christianity, that we are justified by faith in Christ, not by works of the Law.

MARTIN LUTHER

When it comes to theological debates, you don't have to look very far to find one. Just scroll through any social media platform and you will quickly discover people who are very passionate about defending what they believe. In fact, I used to be one of those people. I'd spend countless hours on Facebook, Instagram, and X (formerly Twitter) arguing about various distinctions in the Christian faith. In hindsight, I realize that many of my arguments were centered on issues that did not compromise the gospel.

Yet this was not the case for Paul. His argument to the Galatians addresses the very core of Christian belief and practice—the gospel. Unlike many debates today, which often get muddled in personal opinion, politics, or tradition, Paul's battle was completely different. This was not a matter of mere theological preference but one of first importance. Paul knew that if the Galatians got the gospel wrong, then they would inevitably get everything else wrong. There is simply no way forward if the gospel is compromised.

This week we will examine Paul's missionary journeys and see firsthand what it's like to stand on the front line of defending the gospel. My prayer is that as we study, we will be encouraged to share the gospel with clarity, conviction, and courage, just like Paul. May we strive to stand against all ideologies and distortions that compromise the one true gospel of Jesus Christ.

Key Terms

Gentile: a person who is not a Jew

Propitiation: the act of Jesus satisfying God's justice by his life, death, and resurrection

Justification: being declared righteous before God

Galatians 2:1–21

WEEK 2 | DAY 1
Galatians 2:1–5

Read Galatians 2. After reading the entire chapter, focus on verses 1–5 and answer the following questions:

- In verse 1, Paul mentions that he went up to Jerusalem again after fourteen years. Can you recall where Paul was ministering during the fourteen years before this? (Hint: Reread Gal. 1:21.)

- With whom does Paul travel to Jerusalem?

- According to verse 2, what is Paul's primary reason for traveling to Jerusalem? Who prompted him to go? With whom does he meet? Why does Paul confer privately with them?

- How does the inclusion of Titus, an uncircumcised Gentile, as one of Paul's travel companions to his meeting with the leaders in Jerusalem highlight the central message of the gospel? Why was this significant for the broader debate about religious requirements for Gentiles who converted to Christianity?

- In verse 4, Paul mentions "false brothers" who infiltrated his meeting. Why does Paul refer to these men in this way? What are they promoting? Why is Paul so concerned about this? What is the potential impact of the false brothers' teaching on the early church?

- In verse 4, Paul contrasts freedom and enslavement. How does his language connect to the overarching theme of grace in Galatians?

Galatians 2:1–21

- What is Paul's response to the false brothers who interfered with his meeting in Jerusalem (v. 5)?

- Paul responds this way "so that the truth of the gospel might be preserved for" the Galatians (v. 5). Yet Paul's words are good for us today too. How does Paul set an example for preserving the truth of the gospel? Why must believers contend for the truth of the gospel?

Personal Reflection

What are some things that you have falsely believed about the gospel? How do false beliefs about the gospel enslave us? How does the truth of God's word help you understand and embrace true freedom, which is found only in Christ?

WEEK 2 | DAY 2

Galatians 2:6–10

Reread Galatians 2. After rereading the entire chapter, focus on verses 6–10 and answer the following questions:

- Paul describes those he met with as "influential" but also adds the caveat that their reputation meant nothing to him because "God shows no partiality" (v. 6). Why does Paul find it necessary to make that caveat, and how does it reinforce the validity of the gospel?

Galatians 2:1–21   37

◘ What was the outcome of Paul's meeting with the leaders in Jerusalem? Did they add anything to the message Paul was preaching?

◘ With whom was Paul supposed to share the gospel (v. 7)?

Did You Know?

In Galatians 2, Paul refers to the same person using two names: Peter and Cephas. "Peter" is the Greek version of the name, while "Cephas" is the Aramaic name. Both mean "rock" and reflect this apostle's foundational role in the early Christian church. Paul uses both names in verses 7–9 in order to underscore the wide range of cultures and languages represented in the early church. Seeing both names in Scripture showcases to readers Paul's pivotal role in bridging the gap between Jewish and Gentile believers.

- In verse 9, Paul mentions ministry partners whom he refers to as "pillars." Who are they? Who are they supposed to share the gospel with?

- Who called Paul and his partners to share the gospel with these groups?

- According to verses 9–10, how do these "pillars" in the faith receive Paul and the gospel message that he preaches? What does their response imply about Paul's message and his authority as an apostle to the Gentiles?

- What did Paul's partners ask him to remember as he continued gospel ministry?

Galatians 2:1–21

◻ Read Romans 15:25–33, 1 Corinthians 16:1–4, and 2 Corinthians 8:9. How do these passages help us understand the Christian call to be unified not only in our understanding of the gospel but also in how we practice the gospel in our daily living?

....
....
....
....

Personal Reflection

The gospel brings unity among the most diverse groups of people, as evidenced by the unity among the apostles. What can we learn from the apostles' example of unity and diversity? How might this practically inform your engagement with believers who have different opinions?

....
....
....
....
....
....
....
....

WEEK 2 | DAY 3
Galatians 2:11–14

Reread Galatians 2. After rereading the entire chapter, focus on verses 11–14 and answer the following questions:

◘ Describe Paul's confrontation with Peter. What prompted Paul to confront him?

◘ Acts 10:1–48 sheds more light on why Peter's behavior warranted Paul's confrontation. Read this passage and then summarize it in your own words.

◘ The Greek word for "hypocrisy" means "play-acting, pretense, [or] outward show."[1] What made Peter's behavior, as recounted in Galatians, hypocritical? How did Peter's behavior affect other believers, including his colaborer Barnabas?

Think on This

Table Fellowship in the Ancient World

Understanding Table Fellowship

In Judaism, table fellowship was a tradition of sharing meals, which not only involved eating with others but was also an expression of shared culture or religion as well as social distinctions.[2] In ancient Jewish society, the people one ate with and the manner of eating actually reflected deeper religious convictions. Strict adherence to dietary restrictions and premeal ceremonial washing were marks of Jewish identity that separated pious Jews from sinful Gentiles.

Christ's Transformation of Table Fellowship

Jesus Christ radically transformed the concept of table fellowship during his earthly ministry. As recorded throughout the Gospels, Jesus was known for his open-table fellowship and often dined with tax collectors, sinners, and others who were marginalized by Jewish society (Mark 2:15–17). He used the table to showcase the radically inclusive nature of God's kingdom. Jesus's meals with those who were deemed unclean and unworthy were a powerful testament to God's grace and redemption. And this practice was an unmistakable rebuke to the religious leaders of that day.

Peter's Compromise and Paul's Rebuke

The ancient practice of table fellowship sets the stage for Peter and Paul's interaction in Galatians 2:11–14, thus helping us understand its significance. After receiving the gospel,

Peter initially practiced open-table fellowship with Gentile believers. However, when certain people like the Judaizers came around, Peter feared criticism and withdrew from eating with these Gentiles. Paul's rebuke of Peter's actions is a sobering moment that underscores the gospel's implications for Christian community and fellowship. Through this public confrontation, Paul makes it clear that the gospel of Jesus Christ demolishes the old barriers of the law and creates a new family that is fully united by faith. This confrontation is just one instance of the early church's struggle to fully grasp and live out the truth of the gospel. And Paul's rebuke serves as a corrective measure to anyone in his time and beyond who would distort the gospel with partiality.

The Practice of Open-Table Fellowship Today

The principles behind table fellowship in the New Testament have lasting significance for the church today. Believers are called to reflect the all-encompassing, boundary-crossing love of Christ. In Christ, we truly experience God's grace in that we are given the privilege of sitting at our Father's table. As you consider the encounter between Peter and Paul in Galatians 2, take a moment to examine your own practices of fellowship. Does your table—whether the physical table in your home or the metaphorical table of your church community—reflect the reality of Christian unity in the gospel, or have you allowed cultural barriers to stand strong?

About Antioch

During Paul's ministry, Antioch was a large city that stood as a prominent hub within the Roman Empire. The city was well-known for its cultural diversity, economic strength, and wide range of religious beliefs. Interestingly, Antioch was located at the intersection of various trade routes, making it a high-traffic area for not only commerce but also religious expansion. Believers today may know of Antioch as the place where "disciples were first called Christians" (Acts 11:26).[3]

Galatians 2:1–21 43

- Why was Paul so adamant about confronting Peter publicly? Ultimately, what is at stake in how Peter's behavior affected the message of the gospel?

- According to Paul, what are the implications of living out the truth of the gospel (v. 14)? What does this mean for believers today? What are some practical ways that you can live out the truth of the gospel?

Personal Reflection

When it comes to being a Christian, it is not enough to simply know and affirm the tenets of the faith. We must conform to it in every aspect of our lives! Think about your life as a follower of Jesus Christ. Are there ways that you might be living inconsistently with the gospel? How can you address these issues? Take a moment to pray and ask for God's guidance and help in those specific areas.

WEEK 2 | DAY 4

Galatians 2:15–16

Reread Galatians 2. After rereading the entire chapter, focus on verses 15–16 and answer the following questions:

- Note the distinctions that Paul makes between Jews and Gentiles (see table 1). Why are Paul's distinctions between Jew and Gentile relevant to his discussion about justification?

Table 1. The differences between Jews and Gentiles according to Galatians 2:15

	Jews	Gentiles
Identity	Jews by birth; seen as the covenant people who received the law of Moses	Non-Jews; not part of the Mosaic covenant by birth
Law	Under the Mosaic law, which includes various ceremonial, moral, and civil rules	Did not adhere to the Mosaic law
Justification	Justified through faith in Jesus Christ, not by works of the law	Justified through faith in Jesus Christ, not by works of the law
Faith and Grace	Called to follow the path of justification by faith alone instead of attaining righteousness through law keeping	Receive God's grace and justification through faith without the need for following the Mosaic law
Redemptive Status	Though privileged with the covenant and law, need faith in Christ for salvation, just like Gentiles	Have equal opportunity for salvation through faith in Christ

- Paul uses the phrase "Gentile sinners" in verse 15. What does this phrase suggest about the general Jewish view of Gentiles at the time? Why is it surprising that Paul, a Jewish believer, uses this phrase in his argument about justification?

- In verse 16, Paul says, "a person is not justified by works of the law but through faith in Jesus Christ." What does the term "justified" mean in this context?

- What are the "works of the law" (v. 16)? How does Paul's statement that "a person is not justified by works of the law" challenge the beliefs of the Jews?

- Why is justification by faith in Jesus Christ such good news for both Jews and Gentiles? What implications does this theological truth have for the unity of the Galatian church and for how we live out our Christian unity today?

Galatians 2:1–21

Personal Reflection

What does it mean to you to be justified by faith in Jesus Christ? How does this truth influence your daily life as a believer? Are there areas of your life where you struggle to live by faith? Are you trying to make yourself right with God by adhering to a set of religious rules or standards? Take time to pray, confessing any attempts to attain justification apart from Christ.

WEEK 2 | DAY 5
Galatians 2:17–21

Reread Galatians 2. After rereading the entire chapter, focus on verses 17–21 and answer the following questions:

- In verse 17, Paul asks a rhetorical question: "But if, in our endeavor to be justified in Christ, we too were found to be sinners, is Christ then a servant of sin?" Read 1 John 1:5–10 and Romans 6:1–2. Is Christ sinful? Does he promote sinfulness? How do these verses help us better understand Paul's point in Galatians 2:17?

- In Galatians 2:18 Paul says, "If I rebuild what I tore down, I prove myself to be a transgressor." How does this statement relate to the concept of turning back to the law after receiving the gospel of grace?

Galatians 2:1–21

- Paul asserts in verse 19 that he lives for God since dying to the law. Read the following passages and then explain how they clarify Paul's point in Galatians 2:19:

  - Romans 3:9–18, 23; 6:23
  - 1 Peter 2:24
  - Hebrews 9:28
  - Romans 5:6–10
  - 2 Corinthians 5:14–21
  - Titus 2:14

- Paul makes four big points in Galatians 2:20. Explain each of these in your own words.

- According verse 20, what does it mean to be "crucified with Christ"? How does the indwelling presence of Christ affect how we navigate daily struggles and temptations?

- Paul ends verse 20 by describing Jesus Christ as the one "who loved me and gave himself for me." How does knowing this truth embolden your faith in Jesus Christ?

- In verse 21, Paul says, "I do not nullify the grace of God." How would one nullify the grace of God? How can believers avoid doing that?

Personal Reflection

What is your greatest struggle with accepting the truth that you cannot earn God's grace? How can you shift your focus from relying on yourself to relying on Christ? What changes might this shift bring about in your thoughts, actions, and spiritual growth?

Week 2 Group Discussion

1. Galatians 2:1–2 tells us that Paul went to Jerusalem because God told him to go. Paul's secondary motivation was to challenge the influence of those who were promoting a false gospel. How does Paul's example help us check our own motivations when sharing the gospel? Why is it important to make sure that our reasons for sharing the gospel and doing ministry are aligned with God's will?

2. In Galatians 2, Paul is adamant that Gentile Christians should not be forced to follow Jewish customs as a means of salvation. How could the principle behind this argument be applied in your church?

3. In what ways have you held cultural preferences to be as important as the gospel? What are some ways you can welcome those who are different into your church while also protecting the truth of the gospel?

4. What can we learn from Paul's boldness in confronting Peter? How should we deal with hypocrisy when we see it in our church leaders or in fellow Christians?

5. Share with the group how knowing that you are justified by faith changed your walk with God. What does it mean to be "crucified with Christ"? How is your new life in Christ different from your life before you followed Christ?

6. Paul says we are made right with God by faith, not by following the law. Why is this so important for Christians to understand? How can getting this wrong lead us to follow rules with the wrong motivations (like earning favor with God) or not caring about God's law at all?

7. Are there times when you try to do things on your own instead of trusting in what Jesus has done? How has this week's study helped you live more by faith through God's grace? Share one practical step you will take this week to apply what you've learned from Galatians 2.

Week 3

THE PROMISE OF FREEDOM
(GALATIANS 3:1–14)

His faith was not his righteousness, but God so rewarded his exercise of faith, as that upon it he reckoned (or imputed) that to him which was his righteousness . . . in whom he believed as revealed unto him in the promise.

MATTHEW POOLE

VIDEO 4

Have you ever been asked, "What were you thinking?" Maybe you made a questionable decision or a flippant remark. I remember the days of my mama asking me this very question when I was a teen. Though it doesn't necessarily prompt a verbal response, it certainly prompts a reflective pause to consider how you might have veered off course.

This is exactly what we see in the opening lines of Galatians 3. Paul's words at the outset of this chapter are mixed with frustration and concern as he confronts the Galatian believers by saying, "O foolish Galatians! Who has bewitched you?" (v. 1). This pointed question isn't just a rebuke but a call to self-examination and realignment with the truth of the gospel.

In this passage, Paul dives into the heart of the debate about the law's ability to save by challenging the Galatians—and us—to reflect on the foundation of our spiritual lives. He's perplexed by their sudden shift to law keeping and, through a series of rhetorical questions, reminds them of the faith that initiated and sustains their lives as believers. Paul's words in this section are seemingly harsh, but at their core, they are a loving plea for the Galatians to return to God's grace.

As we reflect on Galatians 3:1–14 this week, I invite you to see yourself in the Galatians' story. Are you foolishly trying to earn what has been freely given? Paul's words serve as a wake-up call that urges apathetic believers to embrace the freedom found by having faith in Jesus Christ, a freedom that truly transcends the confines of the law. Through faith in Christ, we are invited into a story of redemption and transformation, a story where we, like the Galatians, are called to live as children of the promise—fully, freely, and fruitfully.

Key Terms

Children of God: those who are adopted into God's family and are thus recipients of his promises

The Mosaic law: rules provided by God to guide and protect human beings

Curse: a declaration of harm or disaster

WEEK 3 | DAY 1
Galatians 3:1–3

Read Galatians 3:1–14. After reading the entire passage, focus on verses 1–3 and answer the following questions:

- Paul starts this passage by calling the Galatians "foolish," thus taking a much stronger approach compared to his more gentle tone in Galatians 1:6 and 1:11. How does this shift in Paul's tone help us understand the gravity of the situation the Galatians were facing? What might this reveal about the urgency of correcting their error?

- The Greek word for "bewitched" in verse 1 means "to give someone the evil eye, to cast a spell over, to fascinate in the original sense of holding someone spellbound by an irresistible power."[1] (Fun fact: This word is not found anywhere else in the New Testament!) What does Paul's use of the word "bewitched" say about the severity of the Galatians' actions and their departure from the truth of the gospel?

- At the end of verse 1, Paul reminds the Galatians that "Jesus Christ was publicly portrayed as crucified" before their eyes. How does focusing on Jesus's crucifixion deter the Galatians from following a false gospel?

- In verse 2, Paul says, "Let me ask you only this: Did you receive the Spirit by works of the law or by hearing with faith?" How does this question help us understand God's grace?

- Paul continues his string of questions in verse 3, saying, "Having begun by the Spirit, are you now being perfected by the flesh?" What does this question reveal about the source of Christian maturity and growth?

- Paul wrote his letter to the Galatians during a time when the first Christian churches were being established. You can find these early accounts recorded in the book of Acts. Read the following passages:

    - Acts 2:1–4
    - Acts 3:6–7

Galatians 3:1–14

- Acts 4:32–35
- Acts 5:12–16
- Acts 8:29
- Acts 16:6–7

How do these passages help us understand what it means to live by faith? More specifically, how do they support the main point Paul is making in Galatians 3:1–3?

Personal Reflection

Paul fiercely confronts the Galatians for turning to human effort for salvation after starting their faith by relying on the Spirit. Have you ever been confronted about an error in your beliefs? How did you respond? As you reflect on Paul's bold approach, what can you learn from his example about addressing errors that change the heart of the gospel?

WEEK 3 | DAY 2

Galatians 3:4–6

Reread Galatians 3:1–14. After rereading the entire passage, focus on verses 4–6 and answer the following questions:

- What questions does Paul ask in these verses? How do these questions help the Galatians realize that they have been following the law instead of faith?

Galatians 3:1–14

- In verse 4, Paul says, "Did you suffer so many things in vain—if indeed it was in vain?" What does this question imply about the value of enduring hardships for the faith? How can experiences of suffering reveal the law's inability to save us and ultimately point us to our need for faith in Christ?

- How does Paul's question in verse 5 help us see that God's work in our lives is based on faith rather than following the law?

- In verse 6, Paul mentions Abraham to the Galatians. Abraham was not well-known to this Gentile audience, but his name would have definitely grabbed their attention because the Judaizers used Abraham to support their argument for continuing the practice of circumcision in the church. How does Paul explain Abraham's righteousness?

- Read Genesis 15:1–21. How does this passage deepen your understanding of the covenant between God and Abraham? How do these verses reinforce Paul's argument to the Galatians about justification by faith alone? Take a look at Genesis 15:6 and explain in your own words how this verse is a key part of Paul's message about faith and righteousness.

- What is the main point Paul is making to the Galatians through his series of questions?

Personal Reflection

How do Paul's questions in these verses remind us to persevere in faith? When we face hard times and are tempted to rely on our own strength or explain away God's miraculous work with human reasoning, how can these verses help us refocus on the grace of God and trust his promises?

WEEK 3 | DAY 3

Galatians 3:7–9

Reread Galatians 3:1–14. After rereading the entire passage, focus on verses 7–9 and answer the following questions:

- According to Paul, who are the true children of Abraham? How does this challenge both the Jews' exclusivism and the Galatians' legalism?

- In verse 8, Paul says, "The Scripture, foreseeing that God would justify the Gentiles by faith, preached the gospel beforehand to Abraham, saying, 'In you shall all the nations be blessed.'" How does the early declaration in Scripture (found in Genesis 12:3) about the nations being blessed through Abraham support Paul's message to the Galatians?

- Why is it important for the Galatians, many of whom were probably Gentiles, to understand that they were not an afterthought in God's plan of redemption but always meant to be included?

- Paul concludes verse 9 by saying that those who are "of faith" are "blessed along with Abraham, the man of faith." What is this blessing, and how does it differ from seeking righteousness through the law?

Galatians 3:1–14

◘ How has the word "blessed" been misused and manipulated today? What does true blessing entail, and how does it extend beyond material prosperity?

◘ How does Paul's argument that faith, not ethnic lineage or adherence to the law, identifies the true children of Abraham reframe the Galatians' understanding of their place in God's family and plan?

Personal Reflection

Have you ever believed that you've earned God's favor by your own efforts, especially in contrast to other, less faithful believers? How can you remind yourself that Jesus secures God's favor for you, just as he did for Abraham and does for all believers?

WEEK 3 | DAY 4

Galatians 3:10–12

Reread Galatians 3:1–14. After rereading the entire passage, focus on verses 10–12 and answer the following questions:

◘ In verse 10, Paul cites Deuteronomy 27:26 to illustrate that relying on the law for justification places one under a curse. Why is attempting to fulfill the law's demands by human effort destined to fail? How does this help you understand the nature of the law itself?

Galatians 3:1–14

- Read the following passages:

  - Deuteronomy 28:15–68 (Yes, I know that's a lot, but stick with me.)
  - Jeremiah 11:3–5
  - James 2:10

  What do these passages say about being under a curse? What does this reveal about the strictness and high demands of the law for achieving righteousness? How is being made right with God through faith different from righteousness achieved through keeping the law?

- When Paul says in verse 11 that "the righteous shall live by faith," he is quoting Habakkuk 2:4. How does this Old Testament verse underpin Paul's argument against legalism? In light of what we've learned about ancient Jewish practices, how are Paul's words here shocking?

◘ In verses 10–12, how does Paul describe the difference between living under the law and living by faith? What are the consequences of each of these? How would you compare a life based on following the law with a life rooted in faith in Christ?

....
....
....
....

◘ So far, Paul has made a clear case for how it is impossible to become right with God by keeping the law. How does knowing that you could never secure righteousness on your own show you the necessity of Christ's sacrifice on the cross and why we must have faith in him in order to be saved?

....
....
....
....

Personal Reflection

In what ways have you felt pressured to relate to God through legalism? Galatians 3:10–12 shows us that relying on the law brings a curse but faith in Christ brings freedom. How does this understanding transform the way you intentionally live out your faith and how you relate to God?

....
....
....

_____
_____
_____
_____
_____
_____
_____

WEEK 3 | DAY 5

Galatians 3:13–14

Reread Galatians 3:1–14. After rereading the entire passage, focus on verses 13–14 and answer the following questions:

◘ In verse 13, Paul states that "Christ redeemed us from the curse of the law by becoming a curse for us." Consider the significance of this act. Theologians call this "substitutionary atonement" and define it as "the work Christ did to earn our salvation by standing in our place in his life and death."[1] How does this help you understand what Christ did for you?

_____
_____

◻ When Paul says, "Cursed is everyone who is hanged on a tree," he is citing Deuteronomy 21:23. How does this passage relate to Christ's crucifixion? What does it mean for Christ to take the curse upon himself, and how does this act fulfill the law?

◻ In verse 14, Paul explains that through Christ's redemption, the blessing of Abraham extends to the Gentiles so that they "might receive the promised Spirit through faith." Think about how God's plan of redemption has been consistent from the time of Abraham up to the time of Jesus. How does this show us that the gospel is for all people to hear?

◻ How does the gift of the Holy Spirit demonstrate God's grace and love and reinforce the idea that salvation is received by faith? (This is a good time to circle back around to Galatians 3:5 and note how Paul is connecting the dots of his argument.)

Galatians 3:1–14

◻ What do verses 13 and 14 reveal about the impact of Christ's redemptive work on Jewish–Gentile relations in the early church? How did Christ's sacrifice on the cross break down barriers between Jews and Gentiles? What does this tell us about the nature of God's kingdom?

Personal Reflection

How does knowing that Christ has redeemed you from the curse of the law and made it possible for you to receive the Spirit through faith affect your sense of identity and your relationship with God? How does the promise of the Spirit and the blessing of Abraham influence your approach to community, worship, and mission?

Week 3 Group Discussion

1. How does Paul's language in Galatians 3:1 reveal his deep concern for the Galatians? How do his words show the urgency of rejecting false teachers and building a defense against false doctrine in our homes and churches?

2. In light of Paul's argument that we are justified by faith and not by the law, how would you explain the role of the law in the life of believers today? How can we rely more on grace than on personal striving?

3. In Galatians 3:13, Paul says that Christ has redeemed us from the curse of the law by becoming a curse for us. How does this exchange—Christ taking on the curse for our sake and granting us his righteousness—deepen our appreciation for the gospel? How can we keep the message of the cross at the forefront of our lives as believers both individually and communally?

4. Take a moment to think about the evidence of the Holy Spirit's work in your life. Share with the group how the Spirit has increased your faith, changed your life, and brought you into closer fellowship with other believers. How does recounting the blessings of the Spirit redirect your focus from self to God?

5. Share with your group a time when you've been tempted to think you can earn God's favor, and discuss how knowing that we can't earn righteousness by following the law helps us resist that kind of temptation.

6. By faith, we are called "sons of Abraham," which also means "daughters"! How does this truth shape our understanding of God's salvific plan? How can our identity as daughters of Abraham motivate us to more readily share the gospel with people of both genders and all ethnicities and backgrounds?

7. How does Paul's teaching this week lead you to examine your own life? Are there any specific areas of your life where you need to stop relying on your own efforts and trust the work of Christ? How can you rely more on the power of the Holy Spirit? Take some time as a group to pray and encourage one another to live in the grace of God.

Week 4

THE PATHWAY TO FREEDOM
(GALATIANS 3:15–24)

When the Law drives you to the point of despair, let it drive you a little farther, let it drive you straight into the arms of Jesus who says: "Come unto me, all ye that labour and are heavy laden, and I will give you rest."

MARTIN LUTHER

VIDEO 5

A few years ago, my husband and I set out on a journey of searching for a new house to purchase. If you've ever waded through the home-buying process, then you're well aware of its complexities. It's definitely not something that I want to go through again anytime soon. But I did see a helpful illustration for Galatians 3:15–22 in this experience. I learned that when the potential buyers finally select a home and it is listed as "under contract," the buyer and seller are protected from the risk of the other party impulsively backing out of the deal. The contract functions as a binding agreement for the sellers to sell and the buyers to buy. This is just what Paul says in Galatians 3:15–22 when he breaks down the immutable nature of God's promises and draws a parallel with human covenants to underscore his point. Much like a real estate contract, no one can cancel or change a ratified covenant.

However, while God's covenant with Abraham was unchanging, the law (which came later) served a different function in God's plan. In Galatians 3, Paul carefully delineates the true purpose of the law. He helps us understand that the law was intended to be a compass of sorts, pointing us to our true Redeemer, Jesus Christ. In this week's teachings, we'll see that Paul is continuing to make a case for righteousness that comes by faith in Jesus Christ. Most importantly, Paul shows us how righteousness by faith has always been the plan, even before the law was given. God's promise to Abraham was made years before the law came (430 years, to be exact), and as significant as the law is, it would never invalidate the promises of God.

This week, I hope that Paul's words will challenge you to think even more deeply about the beauty of God's redemptive plan. May you be encouraged to walk unashamed in the grace that God has extended to you, knowing that his desire to grant you salvation has been and always will be a part of the plan.

Key Terms

Offspring: a child or descendant

Guardian: someone who watches, guides, or teaches a child

Heir: a person who is entitled to something after the death of a relative

WEEK 4 | DAY 1
Galatians 3:15–16

Read Galatians 3:15–24. After reading the entire passage, focus on verses 15–16 and answer the following questions:

◻ Paul begins this section of Galatians by comparing God's promises to a human covenant in order to show their seriousness and unchanging nature. Why do you think Paul chose this analogy, and how does it help us understand the promise God made to Abraham and its lasting impact?

◻ In verse 16, Paul points out that the term "offspring" used in God's promise to Abraham is singular, not plural. Why is this significant? According to the text, who is this offspring?

- Let's connect the dots here: If God has promised to bless Abraham and his offspring, then who else shares in the promises of God? How does this connection impact us today?

- Reflecting on the promise made to Abraham and seeing it come to life in Jesus gives us an all-around view of God's redemptive plan. How does seeing this connection between the Old and New Testaments deepen your understanding of God's plan for salvation?

- Look at the ways that Christ is the fulfillment of the promise made to Israel in Abraham (table 2). How does this shape your understanding of who the true Israel is?

Table 2. Christ's fulfillment of the promise to Abraham

Promise to Abraham	Fulfillment in Christ
Land (Gen. 12:1; 15:18)	Because of Christ, we have an eternal inheritance, which is the kingdom of God (Matt. 5:5; Heb. 11:16)
Descendants and nation (Gen. 12:2; 15:5)	Faith in Christ creates a spiritual nation, the church (Gal. 3:29; 1 Pet. 2:9)
Great name (Gen. 12:2)	Christ has been given the name above every name (Phil. 2:9–10)
Blessing to all nations (Gen. 12:3; 22:18)	Christ brings the blessing of salvation to all peoples (Gal. 3:8; Matt. 28:19)
Kingship and kingdom (Gen. 17:6, 16)	Christ, the King of kings, establishes an everlasting kingdom (Luke 1:32–33; Rev. 19:16)
Everlasting covenant (Gen. 17:7)	Christ sealed the new covenant of forgiveness for sin with his blood (Luke 22:20; Heb. 13:20)
Personal relationship with God (Gen. 17:7–8)	Christ gives access to a personal relationship with God as Father (John 1:12–13; Gal. 4:4–7)

Personal Reflection

The Abrahamic promise and its fulfillment in Christ is both personally and communally significant for believers today. How does being a recipient of this promise through faith in Christ affect your daily life, decision-making, and spiritual growth? In what practical ways does this assurance of God's faithfulness to his children inform your actions and interactions as a Christian?

_____
_____
_____
_____
_____
_____
_____
_____
_____
_____
_____
_____

WEEK 4 | DAY 2
Galatians 3:17–18

Reread Galatians 3:15–24. After rereading the entire passage, focus on verses 17–18 and answer the following questions:

- In verse 17, Paul explains that the law came 430 years *after* God's covenant with Abraham. This means that the law does not cancel God's covenant. How does this truth show the permanence of God's covenantal promises?

- In your own words, describe how the law (given hundreds of years after the covenant) relates to God's promises. What was its purpose?

- Can the promises of God be attained by works, or are they received by faith? How does distinguishing between righteousness by faith and righteousness by works of the law help us understand our relationship with God and how we receive his promises?

- In verse 18, Paul contrasts what it means to receive an inheritance by law with what it means to receive an inheritance by promise. Consider the fundamental differences between earning something by adherence to a set of rules and receiving it as a gift. What does this distinction tell us about the nature of the inheritance promised to Abraham and his offspring?

- Paul is clear that our ultimate inheritance comes through God's promise, not through keeping the law. What do you think this emphasis on promise over law tells us about the character of God and his desires for our relationship with him?

Galatians 3:15–24

◻ In Western culture, where we are told to do more and try harder, how does this section of Scripture bring you comfort? Specifically, what does it tell you about what God really wants from those who seek him?

....
....
....
....

Personal Reflection

God's promise to Abraham came long before the law, and even though the law was given 430 years later, it did not cancel his promise. Instead, it brought his plan closer to fulfillment. Can you think of a time when you've experienced broken promises in your life? How does reflecting on God as the eternal promise keeper—who never breaks his word, even when we don't fully understand his plan—encourage you to trust him more deeply in your current season of life?

....
....
....
....
....
....
....

WEEK 4 | DAY 3
Galatians 3:19–20

Reread Galatians 3:15–24. After rereading the entire passage, focus on verses 19–20 and answer the following questions:

- According to verse 19, what was the purpose of the law, and how does it relate to the promise made to Abraham's offspring? (Note: It may be helpful to read this verse in the NLT or CSB.)

- Paul states that the law "was added because of transgressions." How does this connection between the law and transgressions help us grasp the purpose of the law? What does this imply about our sinful nature and the need for guidance through the law?

Galatians 3:15–24

- Paul also notes that the law was put in place through angels and intermediaries (e.g., Moses). What does this imply about the nature of the law in contrast to the nature of the Abrahamic promise? Specifically, compare God's delivery of the promise with his delivery of the law (see table 3).

Table 3. The promise versus the law

Promise	Law
Made initially when Abram was called (Gen. 12:1-3)	Given 430 years after the promise
Unconditional; received by faith	Conditional; based on obedience
God ↓ Abraham	God ↓ Intermediaries/Moses ↓ Humanity
Establishes a covenant with the promise of blessing	Exposes transgressions and guides behavior

- In verse 20, Paul says more about intermediaries and the law. What is the role of an intermediary? How does the intermediary's role help us understand God's role in the covenant? Paul specifically says that "God is one." How does this emphasize God's unique role in both giving and fulfilling his promises?

- In light of what Paul has said about the law's role, what conclusions can you draw about its limitations? How does recognizing these limitations help us see the bigger picture of God's plan for salvation?

- What does Christ's role as the only mediator for God's promise—as opposed to the multiple mediators of the law—tell us about the uniqueness of Christ's role in God's plan for salvation? How does having one mediator change the way we view the promise of salvation?

Personal Reflection

God gave us the law to guide and protect us in much the same way that parents set rules to protect their children from harm. Just like a parent's rules come from a place of care and concern, so does God's law. How does viewing the law in this light help you appreciate the loving nature of your heavenly Father?

....

....

....

....

....

....

....

....

....

....

....

....

....

....

WEEK 4 | DAY 4
Galatians 3:21–22

Reread Galatians 3:15–24. After rereading the entire passage, focus on verses 21–22 and answer the following questions:

- What do verses 21–22 say about the relationship between the law and the promises of God? Use the table below to write out the key elements of each as described in these verses.

Promise	Law

Galatians 3:15–24 85

◻ In this passage, Paul tackles the question of whether the law conflicts with God's promises, concluding that it does not. Read the following Scripture passages. How do these passages affirm Paul's argument and help you understand the harmony of the law and the promises of God?

- Matthew 5:17–20

- Romans 3:20–23

- Romans 3:31

- Romans 7:7–13

- Hebrews 7:18–19

- How does Paul describe the law's role in accessing righteousness and new life in verse 21? What does this tell us about the law's limitations?

- In verse 22, Paul says that Scripture declares everyone a prisoner of sin. How does knowing that we are all "imprisoned" by sin help us understand the role of faith in our lives? How does believing in Jesus change our relationship with and status before God?

- Let's look at verse 22 again. Paul explains that Scripture has imprisoned everything under sin, which reveals our inability to achieve righteousness on our own. Though Paul is specifically referring to the law of Moses, we can also think of "Scripture" as the whole Bible. How does studying Scripture increase our awareness of sin and need for grace as well as remind us of God's promises?

Galatians 3:15–24

◻ What is the condition for receiving the promises of God? Who are the recipients of God's promises?

_____
_____
_____

Personal Reflection

What do these verses tell us about how believers should view the law? Specifically, how does understanding the purpose of the law change your approach to studying the Bible and applying it to your life? What, if anything, should you do differently as you seek to know God's word?

_____
_____
_____
_____
_____
_____
_____
_____
_____

WEEK 4 | DAY 5
Galatians 3:23–24

Reread Galatians 3:15–24. After rereading the entire passage, focus on verses 23–24 and answer the following questions:

- How does Paul explain the purpose of the law (v. 23)? Specifically, how does Paul describe the period before "faith came"?

- Paul likens the law to a guardian who took care of God's people until Christ's arrival (v. 24). How does this metaphor clarify the law's purpose? What does this metaphor say about the function of the law in the lives of believers before the coming of Christ?

Galatians 3:15–24

◘ The transition from being under the law to being justified by faith is a big deal! How does this transition shift the way believers relate to God?

◘ In what ways do you think the law, acting as a guardian, prepares hearts and minds for the Savior? Identify specific aspects of or commands within the law that hint at the need for Christ. Read the following passages to help you answer this question:

- Romans 3:20
- Hebrews 10:1
- Psalm 19:7

◘ Take a moment to reflect on your life before knowing Christ and believing in him. How did living under the law feel during that time? How did coming to saving faith in Jesus Christ change your view of the law?

Personal Reflection

Many of us have often viewed the law negatively and considered it to be at odds with the grace we experience in Jesus. But according to Paul, the law is not bad. The law was given to us as a guardian to steer and protect us. One of my mentors referred to the law as a "reflection of God's heart."[1] How does God use both the law and faith to showcase his love for us and lead us into deeper communion with him?

Think on This

Faith: Our Response, Not Our Achievement

Unpacking Galatians leads us to a life-changing truth about how we reconcile and connect with God—that it's all through faith. However, we must be careful not to turn our faith into a work. It is not our act of believing that saves us; it is Jesus who saves. Believing in Christ is not a task that we check off to earn favor with God or salvation. It's not about the size or strength of our faith. The person with a seed of faith in Jesus is no less saved than a person with tons of faith. The truth is, when we think of faith as an act that saves us, we mistakenly place the spotlight on ourselves and our efforts rather than on Jesus and his incredible sacrifice.

Viewing faith as a sacred response to what Jesus has done instead of something that we think we can do to impress God helps us rightly see Jesus as the real hero of our salvation story. Thus, our faith is simply an acknowledgment that Jesus is the only one who can make us right with God. Through his life, death, burial, and resurrection, Jesus has done everything needed to truly be declared righteous, and by faith we are simply recipients of that righteousness.

The letter to the Galatians is a clarion call to focus on Jesus. Paul is reminding us that if we could have fixed our relationship with God on our own, then Jesus died for nothing (Gal. 2:21). I pray that, throughout this study, you are reminded that true faith is a response, not an achievement. By responding in faith, we can live freely in the grace of God and not worry about whether we're "doing" faith right or if we "have enough" faith to be saved. Our faith, no matter how small, is simply a response to the real source of our hope and salvation—Jesus Christ.

Week 4 Group Discussion

1. Paul uses the example of a human covenant in Galatians 3:15 to illustrate the permanence of God's promises. Why do you think Paul chose to emphasize the unchanging nature of God's covenant with Abraham by using this example? Share with your group how God, in his faithfulness, has built up your trust in him, especially during challenging times.

2. In Galatians 3:16, Paul highlights that the promise made by God was to Abraham's "seed," referring specifically to Christ. What does this reveal about God's design and intention from the very beginning of his covenant? How does recognizing Jesus as the focal point of God's promises transform the way we read the Old Testament?

3. Discuss how the law revealed sin in your own life and led you to faith in Christ. As you reflect on your journey, share how living under grace rather than the law has refined and deepened your personal relationship with God.

4. Discuss how understanding the law as a guardian changes our perspective on its purpose. How does this insight help us appreciate the law as a part of God's grand narrative of salvation?

5. How does the Christian principle of justification by faith challenge other religious views on achieving righteousness? In what ways has knowing that you are justified by faith directly affected your relationship with believers and nonbelievers?

6. How does understanding that our inheritance comes from God's promise rather than the law influence our identity as believers? Discuss the freedom and assurance that comes from being heirs according to God's promise.

7. Reflect on times when you have leaned toward legalism instead of living by faith. How does Galatians 3:15–24 speak to those experiences? Share ways we can encourage one another to embrace faith over legalism in our walk with Christ.

8. What are the implications of being under the guardianship of the law before coming to faith in Christ? How does transitioning from the guardianship of the law to the freedom of faith in Christ encourage us to live differently? Share how this transition influences our understanding of discipline, obedience, and grace.

Week 5

THE IDENTITY OF FREEDOM
(GALATIANS 3:25–29)

Conversion enables me to answer the most basic of all human questions, "Who am I?" and to say, "In Christ I am a son of God. In Christ I am united to all the redeemed people of God, past, present, and future. In Christ I discover my identity. In Christ I find my feet. In Christ I come home."

JOHN STOTT

In today's culture, the search for identity often takes us down interesting paths. From achievements in our careers to the social circles we run in, our identity quickly and easily become defined by worldly standards.

"She's the new chief of staff at the agency. I hear that she graduated from an Ivy League institution. She's a real go-getter."

"Oh yeah! I remember him. He goes golfing every Friday with the mayor. They're members of the same fraternity!"

"The Smiths are real entrepreneurs. Started their tech company three years ago and already generating over seven figures annually. Now they're teaching everyone else how they did it on Instagram."

While such success can seem very alluring, it doesn't take long before we find ourselves feeling dissatisfied, empty, and alone. But Galatians 3:25–29 can help us think biblically about our individual and communal identity. It teaches us that our true identity is not grounded in what we achieve or the groups we are part of, but in our relationship with Christ.

According to Paul, with the coming of Christ, believers transition from an indirect relationship with God to a direct relationship with God. This transition changes not just how we approach and relate to God but also how we are identified by him. In Christ, we are now children of God through faith, and our newfound status is not based on the benchmarks of society but solely on Christ. In Christ, the usual divisions that separate people are dismantled, and believers are united under a new identity that surpasses all worldly distinctions.

This week, we peel back the layers to further uncover not only our identity as children of God but also our identity as heirs of the promise made to Abraham.

Key Terms

Baptism: a ceremony in which one is initiated into the visible church through sprinkling, pouring, or immersing in water in the name of the triune God as a sign of covenantal faith

Union with Christ: spiritual joining with Christ

Inheritance: valuable possessions that are passed down to others after the death of the owner

Ultimately, we are not defined by our past actions, societal roles, or ethnic backgrounds, but by our position as God's children and heirs of his promise. And if you don't know, this is wonderful news! No longer do we have to look to the world for belonging and purpose; we can look to Jesus and find true freedom in him.

Galatians 3:25–29 challenges us to reexamine the basis of our identity. Go ahead and ask yourself this: Am I ultimately finding my value in accolades, social status, or influence? Or am I finding my value in Christ? This week of our study will help you confidently respond to the latter question with a resounding yes!

WEEK 5 | DAY 1
Galatians 3:25

Read Galatians 3:25–29. After reading the entire passage, focus on verse 25 and answer the following questions:

- Earlier in Galatians, Paul helped us understand the function of the law by likening it to a guardian. What conclusion does Paul now draw regarding the role of the law in verse 25?

- Paul's statement that "faith has come" (v. 25) points to a significant transition in human history that was brought about by Christ's fulfillment of the law. In order to fully understand Paul's point, we need to examine several passages of Scripture.

(a) First, read the following:

- Exodus 19:5–6
- Leviticus 20:26
- Deuteronomy 6:17–18
- Leviticus 19:18
- Romans 3:20

How did the law, given to Moses on Mount Sinai, help Israel relate to God?

(b) Now read the following passages and note how each prophet hints at a new way of relating to the law:

- Jeremiah 31:31–34
- Ezekiel 36:26–27
- Isaiah 2:2–4

(c) Finally, read Matthew 5:17–20. Here Jesus addresses his relationship with the law and the prophets. How do Jesus's words help us understand the connection between the Old and New Testaments? (Fun fact: The word "testament" is simply another word for "covenant." Thus, another way of framing this question is by asking how Jesus is the bridge between God's former covenant with his people and God's new covenant with his people.)

Did You Know?

In Galatians 3, Paul uses the term *paidagōgos* to describe the role of the law as a guardian. In Greek and Roman culture, a *paidagōgos* was "a boy leader whose duty was to conduct a boy or youth to and from school and to superintend his conduct."[1] It is important to note that the *paidagōgos* was not a teacher. In fact, the primary responsibility of the *paidagōgos* was guiding and supervising, not instructing. Thus, this person functioned much like a nanny who provides round-the-clock supervision and protection for a child until the parent returns to get him or her.

Paul creatively employs this analogy to show how the law served as a guardian for God's people, guiding them until the arrival of Christ. Just as the *paidagōgos* supervised a child until an age of maturity, the law was given to guide, protect, and prepare God's people for the Messiah. With the coming of Christ, believers are no longer under the supervision of the *paidagōgos* (i.e., the law) because they have reached maturity of faith in Christ, which is, in essence, the true fulfillment of the law's intent.

This analogy not only helped the Galatians understand Paul's message but also underscored the real purpose of the law. Though the law played a crucial role in God's redemptive history, it was never the ultimate means of salvation. The true Savior is and has always been Jesus Christ.

▫ How does tracing Christ's fulfillment of the law show that faith in Christ is sufficient to declare a sinner righteous before God?

Personal Reflection

I've often heard people say that to fully grasp the good news of the gospel, you first need to understand the bad news. That's how the law works—it reveals our guilt and sinfulness, but it also leads us to trust in Christ instead of ourselves. Have you ever experienced a moment when bad news in your life ultimately led to something good? In what ways does recognizing your inability to keep the law draw you even closer to Christ?

WEEK 5 | DAY 2
Galatians 3:26

Reread Galatians 3:25–29. After rereading the entire passage, focus on verse 26 and answer the following questions:

◘ How does Paul describe the new identity that believers have in Christ (v. 26)?

◘ Table 4 (see next page) compares worldly identity labels with Christian ones. Are there any labels you have regularly found yourself adopting? How does embracing your identity in Christ challenge or replace worldly labels? How does identifying with Christ first and foremost bring freedom and peace for believers?

Table 4. Worldly identity labels versus Christian identity labels

Worldly Identity Labels	Christian Identity Labels
Success vs. failure	Loved unconditionally
Insider vs. outsider	Belong to God's family
Wealthy vs. poor	Heir of God's kingdom
Popular vs. unnoticed	Known intimately by God
Strong vs. weak	Empowered by the Holy Spirit

- Do you think of yourself as a "son of God"? How does seeing yourself as part of God's family influence your thoughts, decisions, and behavior on a day-to-day basis?

....

....

Galatians 3:25–29

Personal Reflection

Think of a time when the labels of society have weighed you down, casting a shadow on who you truly are in Christ. How did you handle that? What practices did you implement or what biblical truths did you meditate on to redirect your focus to your Christ-centered identity? If you are still presently struggling in this area, take a moment to stop and pray. Ask God to help you live as he has called you and not as the world sees fit.

WEEK 5 | DAY 3

Galatians 3:27

Reread Galatians 3:25–29. After rereading the entire passage, focus on verse 27 and answer the following questions:

- In verse 27, Paul connects being "baptized into Christ" with having "put on Christ." What does this tell us about the symbolic purpose of baptism? Read Romans 6:3–4, Colossians 2:12, and 2 Corinthians 5:17. Based on these passages, do you think baptism is just a meal ticket to get into heaven, or does it symbolize something deeper?

- In Romans 13:11–14, Paul tells believers to "put on the Lord Jesus Christ." How does Paul's message in this passage connect with Galatians 3:27? How does it deepen your understanding of what it means to live a life that reflects Christ?

Galatians 3:25–29

- How does "putting on Christ" affect the way you perceive your identity and abilities? How does understanding your union with Christ influence your approach to the challenges and opportunities of life?

- Identify specific areas in your life where Christ needs to be more evident. How can you intentionally "put on" Christ more fully in your daily actions and decisions?

- The call to "put on Christ" is not just an individual one but also a communal one. How does this shared identity in Christ foster deeper unity and greater fellowship among believers in your church?

- The concept of "putting on" is central in both Galatians 3:27 and Ephesians 6:10–18. Explore the similarities between these two passages. What do they teach us about the nature of our Christian identity?

Personal Reflection

In Galatians 3:27, Paul likens Christ to a garment that we are to put on daily. Think about the functions of clothing: Our clothes cover and cling to us. Our clothes can even serve as an identifying marker (e.g., women wear dresses and medical professionals wear scrubs). God looks upon us as children covered in Christ—redeemed, spotless, beautiful children! How does this truth bring you comfort and a sense of freedom?

Galatians 3:25–29 *105*

WEEK 5 | DAY 4
Galatians 3:28

Reread Galatians 3:25–29. After rereading the entire passage, focus on verse 28 and answer the following questions:

🟧 In Galatians 3:25–29, Paul addresses divisions among the Galatians. Let's take a moment to jump back to the beginning of this study, where we briefly explored the history of Galatia (see p. 16). What factors might have led Paul to address these divisions?

_____
_____
_____
_____

🟧 According to verse 28, we are all united in Christ Jesus. What distinctions does Paul say no longer determine our standing?

_____
_____
_____
_____

◘ Why do you think Paul mentions these specific divisions? Left unchecked, what were the potential implications for these divisions on the early church?

◘ It is really important to grasp the essence of what Paul is communicating in this verse. Take a moment to explore the difference between divisions and distinctions. What does verse 28 say about being united in Christ while also recognizing God-given distinctions?

◘ Consider the distinctiveness of the people in your Christian community. How has diversity led to growth and edification in your church rather than division? (Hint: Ephesians 4:1–13 might help you answer this question.)

◘ Similarly to Galatians 3:28, in Ephesians 2:14–16, Paul points out that Christ "has made [Jews and Gentiles] one and has broken down in his flesh the dividing wall of hostility." Consider some of the barriers in our society that have divided people. How does the gospel break these down?

Galatians 3:25–29

....
....
....

Personal Reflection

Paul's words to the Galatians in this verse were probably extremely shocking. He was challenging their very way of life and showing them how the gospel changes everything. And his challenge is just as relevant for believers today. How does Galatians 3:28 confront the stereotypes and prejudices in our society and even our churches?

....
....
....
....
....
....
....
....
....
....
....

WEEK 5 | DAY 5
Galatians 3:29

Reread Galatians 3:25–29. After rereading the entire passage, focus on verse 29 and answer the following questions:

- Paul brings his argument that began in Galatians 3:6 full circle with verse 29. How do these two verses connect to one another?

- In verse 29, Paul uses an if-then statement to clarify the condition that make the Galatians (and all believers) heirs of the promise to Abraham. What is this condition? What is the result of meeting this condition?

- How does this promise specifically affect the Galatians, who were not of Jewish descent and were unfamiliar with the law?

Galatians 3:25–29

- How does realizing that the Gentile Galatians are now a part of Abraham's offspring (through faith) transform the Jews' understanding of what it means to be part of God's family? How does this support Paul's overarching argument that righteousness can be received only by faith instead of by performing works of the law?

- In the Old Testament, an inheritance was often a material blessing, such as land, but in the New Testament, we are told that believers have a spiritual inheritance because they are heirs of God's promise. How does this shift from the physical to spiritual show us what truly matters in God's kingdom?

- Let's examine verse 29 in light of Romans 8:15–17. How do Paul's words to both the Galatians and the Romans show us that the inheritance we receive in Christ extends beyond material and earthly possessions and encompasses eternal and spiritual blessing?

Personal Reflection

Galatians 3:29 states that those who belong to Christ are considered Abraham's offspring and consequently are "heirs according to [the] promise." How does seeing this connection between God's promise to Abraham and its fulfillment in Christ help you embrace the freedom that comes with being in Christ?

Week 5 Group Discussion

1. As believers, Christ is central to our identity. Above all else, we are followers of Christ. Does knowing this truth influence your daily life? If so, how? If not, how can you begin to embrace your identity in Christ in practical ways?

2. Galatians 3:28 speaks strongly against divisions among believers. Are there any barriers, perhaps unrecognized or ignored, that are hindering unity in your church? What steps can you collectively begin to take to dismantle these barriers? How can you intentionally foster a church culture that brings healing to divided spaces and builds bridges across separating lines?

3. Galatians 3:29 speaks of our spiritual heritage by declaring that we are heirs of God's promises. How does recognizing this shared spiritual heritage foster a greater sense of unity in your church? Are there ways your church could focus more on spiritual heritage as opposed to cultural heritage?

4. What are some practical ways that believers can demonstrate unity and love in society at large as a means of healing divisions?

5. Are there any people in your life from whom you differ greatly? Perhaps you share starkly different political views, or maybe you are ethnically and culturally different. How does the call to unity in Galatians 3:25–29 shape your approach to relationships with people inside and outside the family of God who feel different from you?

6. Galatians 3:25–29 not only shapes our thoughts on what it means to be unified as believers but also provides a strong framework for equality among believers. Do you see this in your church? If not, how can you cultivate a culture of biblical equality?

Week 6

HEIRS OF FREEDOM
(GALATIANS 4:1–31)

Our adoption by God as his children, through Jesus Christ, is the highest privilege that the gospel offers.

J. I. PACKER

As much as I love books, I must say that I love the people who write books all the more. I have so much admiration for those who commit to the work of writing. One of my favorite authors is J. K. Rowling, who wrote the well-known Harry Potter series. There's something about her style of writing that just makes the words jump off the page.

As we've seen all throughout our study of Galatians, Paul is not just a teacher of rich theological truths—he is a masterful writer. This week, we will see Paul's writing in action again as he uses analogy and allegory to clarify complex ideas and share the gospel in a clear and accessible way.

Specifically, Paul uses this portion of his letter to help the Galatians remember their spiritual journey from the outset of their faith to the present moment of Paul's writing. To grab their attention, Paul skillfully likens their spiritual growth to the physical growth of children who are reaching a stage of freedom. He notes that as adopted children of God, the Galatians are no longer under the strict guardianship of the law, but rather have freedom because of God's grace. This might paint a pretty picture in your mind right now, but when Paul employs this analogy, he is using it to show his grief over the Galatians' regression into old patterns by clinging to Jewish laws and rituals.

Further, Paul employs another literary device, allegory, by recounting the story of Sarah and Hagar. This illustration supports Paul's robust theological argument and also provides a vivid depiction of two paths: one leading to freedom and the other leading to bondage. As we dig into this week's study, may we see the beauty of Paul's words and, much more importantly, of our freedom in Christ.

Key Terms

Adoption: God's bringing of human beings into his family and giving them all the rights and privileges of that family

"Abba Father": a personal and loving name for calling on God

Covenant: a binding agreement between two parties

WEEK 6 | DAY 1
Galatians 4:1–7

Read Galatians 4. After reading the entire chapter, focus on verses 1–7 and answer the following questions:

▫ In this passage, Paul uses a metaphor of a child heir. Though the child has an inheritance, he does not have access to it. How is this similar to living under the law?

Did You Know?

In ancient Roman culture, the heir, usually the eldest son, was first in line to inherit the father's estate. However, while the heir was a child, he had no legal rights and practically no control over his inheritance. At this time, the legal status of the child wasn't much different from that of a slave—the child had no autonomy and was under the complete authority of the male head of the household. Generally, a child remained under this status until he was formally released by the father or guardian upon reaching an age of maturity.[1]

- The "elementary principles" Paul refers to in Galatians 4:3 are probably the religious and cultural underpinnings of both Jewish and Gentile worlds during the first century, namely, the legalistic religious system and pagan rituals that enslaved Jews and Gentiles respectively. What are some "elementary principles" in our post-Christian society today?

- Reflect on the phrase "the fullness of time" (v. 4). What does it tell us about God's timing and plan regarding Christ's sacrifice for sin?

- Consider the significance of Jesus being "born of woman, born under the law" (v. 4). How does this truth shape your understanding of who Christ is? Specifically, what does this say about Christ's humanity and his obligation to keep the law?

Galatians 4:1–31

◘ According to verses 4–5, how does a person get adopted into God's family?

◘ Paul begins verse 6 with the phrase "because you are sons." What does God do for (or perhaps who does he send to) those in his family?

◘ How does the Spirit confirm our adoption into God's family?

◘ Reflect on the transition from slavery to sonship as mentioned by Paul in verse 7. What do we forfeit when we turn back to slavery by practicing works of the law? How does this regression affect our identity and how we relate to God?

Personal Reflection

In what ways have you experienced a shift from feeling like a slave under the law to experiencing the freedom and identity of being an adopted daughter in Christ? How does understanding your identity as a child of God influence your daily life, choices, and relationships with God and others?

....
....
....
....
....
....
....
....
....
....
....
....
....

Galatians 4:1–31

WEEK 6 | DAY 2
Galatians 4:8–11

Reread Galatians 4. After rereading the entire chapter, focus on verses 8–11 and answer the following questions:

◻ Read the following passages:

- 2 Chronicles 13:9
- Isaiah 37:19
- Jeremiah 2:11; 5:7; 16:20
- 1 Corinthians 8:4

Consider how these passages help you understand Paul's words "enslaved to those that by nature are not gods" in Galatians 4:8. Specifically, how does Galatians 4:8 describe our spiritual state before truly knowing God?

◘ How does Galatians 4:9 depict the the transformation we experience when we come to know God? According to this verse, what is the significance of both knowing God and being known by God?

◘ What concerns are raised in the latter part of verse 9 about returning to "the weak and worthless elementary principles of the world"? Why might this regression be problematic?

◘ In verse 10, Paul mentions the observance of "days and months and seasons and years." Because the Galatians had turned to the Jewish ritual of circumcision, it is probable that they had also turned to Jewish calendar rituals. Why would the practice of observing Jewish holy days be a potential danger for the Galatians? How does such observance relate to being enslaved to elementary principles?

Galatians 4:1–31 121

- How does adhering to holy days and rituals reflect more of a reliance on external practices than a deeper, faith-based relationship with God?

- In verse 11, Paul expresses concern that his efforts with the Galatians might have been "in vain." Why do you think Paul is concerned that his work among them could be wasted? Consider what this reveals about his hopes and expectations for their spiritual growth. (Hint: For more information about Paul's ministry, see 1 Cor. 15:58; Phil. 2:16; 1 Thess. 3:5.)

- How does Paul's concern regarding his laboring among the Galatians highlight the responsibilities and emotional investment of discipling? How does Paul's example of laboring with the Galatians encourage or challenge you in your discipling of other believers?

Personal Reflection

Pause for a moment to consider the challenges that new believers or even seasoned believers might face in maintaining their spiritual growth and avoiding backsliding. How can Galatians 4:8–11 help us understand and navigate our own spiritual journeys, especially in the face of cultural pressures that might pull us away from the faith?

Galatians 4:1–31

WEEK 6 | DAY 3
Galatians 4:12–20

Reread Galatians 4. After rereading the entire chapter, focus on verses 12–20 and answer the following questions:

▫ In verse 12, Paul tells the Galatians to "become as I am," meaning free from the requirements of the Jewish law and living by faith in Christ. How does Paul's willingness to set aside Jewish customs to relate to the Galatians (who are Gentiles) demonstrate his love and commitment to them? What does this reveal about the nature of his relationship with them?

....
....
....
....

▫ Look closely at verse 13. What does Paul say about the circumstances that led him to preach to the Galatians? How might these circumstances have influenced his message or approach?

....
....
....
....

- How did the Galatians respond to Paul when he was ill (v. 14)? What does their reaction say about their understanding of community and compassion in the church?

- In verse 15, Paul says the Galatians would have "gouged out [their] eyes" for him as an expression of their deep devotion and gratitude when they first received the gospel (v. 15). How does this strong language reflect the Galatians' initial joy and sense of blessedness in accepting Paul's message? What might Paul's statement about their willingness to gouge out their eyes tell us about the impact of the gospel on their lives?

- Take a look at verse 16. What tension does Paul highlight between telling the truth and maintaining relationships? Why do you think Paul felt the need to directly address this issue?

- In verse 17, Paul warns about others who "make much of [the Galatian believers], but for no good purpose." What are the dangers of such influences within a

Galatians 4:1–31

church community? How can believers discern between genuine and manipulative praise?

- What does verse 18 say are proper reasons for being valued or esteemed in a Christian community? What criteria do you think makes esteem "for a good purpose"?

- In verse 19, Paul uses another powerful metaphor—childbirth—to describe his feelings for the Galatians. What does this metaphor reveal about Paul's emotional and physical investment and his expectations for the Galatians' spiritual growth?

- How does verse 20 shed light on the challenges of trying to disciple someone who lives far away from you?

Personal Reflection

Responsibly discipling other believers is not for the faint of heart. Paul's ministry to the Galatians is a realistic example of the highs and lows that come with discipleship. How does Galatians 4:12–20 illustrate the earnest care and deep emotional connection Paul had for the Galatians? What can we learn from his approach to handling the joys and challenges of discipling?

Galatians 4:1–31 127

WEEK 6 | DAY 4
Galatians 4:21–27

Reread Galatians 4. After rereading the entire chapter, focus on verses 21–27 and answer the following questions (see table 5 for help):

Table 5. Two covenants: Earthly bondage and heavenly freedom (Gal. 4:21–27)

Covenant	Status	Key Characteristics
Old (Hagar) = **Mount Sinai** = **Present Jerusalem**	Bondage/slavery	• Enslaved with her children; represents the Mosaic covenant and the earthly city • Symbolizes the old covenant, its bondage, and the earthly Jerusalem, thus emphasizing the law's limitations
New (Sarah) = **Christ** = **Jerusalem above**	Freedom and promise	• Free; represents new life in Christ and the heavenly city • Symbolizes the new covenant, freedom in Christ, and the promise of the heavenly inheritance for believers, emphasizing the promise of spiritual inheritance and eternal life

- What question does Paul ask about the law in verse 21? What does this question reveal about the Galatians' understanding of or attitudes toward the law?

- In verse 22, Paul mentions Abraham's two sons, who were born to different mothers. What details does Paul provide about these sons in this verse? How do these details support Paul's argument about freedom in Christ versus bondage under the law?

- In verse 23, Paul explains that Abraham's two sons were also born in different ways: one according to the flesh (i.e., through human effort) and the other through God's promise. How does this distinction help illustrate Paul's teaching on the power of God's promises versus the futile efforts of humans?

- In verse 24, Paul uses the story of Abraham's two sons as an allegory about two covenants. Who are the two women associated with these covenants, and what are the characteristics of the covenants? How does Paul use this allegory to support his argument about freedom in Christ versus bondage under the law?

Galatians 4:1–31

- In verse 25, Paul links Hagar with Mount Sinai and the "present Jerusalem." Remember that Mount Sinai was where God gave the law to Israel. Paul describes Mount Sinai and the present Jerusalem as being in slavery. If adherence to the law is a characteristic of both places, what is Paul implying about the spiritual state of those who have not turned to Jesus in faith?

- During the time of Paul's writing to the Galatians, Jerusalem was under Roman rule. In light of this, what connection is Paul making between Hagar, Mount Sinai, and the present Jerusalem?

- Paul references "Jerusalem above" in verse 26. How does this contrast with his earlier reference to Jerusalem? What does this imply about the nature of the new covenant?

◻ In verse 27, Paul quotes Isaiah 54:1. Why do you think he chose that particular passage? How does it contribute to his overall argument about the covenant and the promise?

....
....
....
....

Personal Reflection

What does the balance between law and grace look like in your life? On one hand, we shouldn't be legalists, but on the other hand, we shouldn't ignore the law altogether. In what ways can you apply the principles of living under the new covenant to your everyday life in order to deepen your faith and daily walk with God?

....
....
....
....
....
....
....

WEEK 6 | DAY 5
Galatians 4:28–31

Reread Galatians 4. After rereading the entire chapter, focus on verses 28–31 and answer the following questions:

- In verse 28, Paul compares the Galatians to Abraham's son Isaac, calling them "children of promise." What does it mean to be a child of the promise in this context? How does this identity contrast with being a child "according to the flesh" (v. 29)?

- In Genesis 21:9, Sarah sees Ishmael mocking Isaac. What parallel does Paul draw between Ishmael's treatment of Isaac and how the Judaizers treat those who are free in Christ? How might this comparison help the Galatians understand the true nature of the opposition they faced from the Judaizers?

- Paul makes a clear distinction between the children of the slave woman (Hagar) and the children of the free woman (Sarah) in verse 30 by quoting Genesis 21:10, which reads, "Cast out the slave woman and her son." How does Paul's use of Genesis 21:10 emphasize the freedom and inheritance promised under the new covenant in Christ?

- Paul concludes that the Galatians are children not of the slave woman but of the free woman. How would understanding this change their perspective or behavior?

Personal Reflection

In your own life, where do you see the conflict between living according to the flesh and living according to the Spirit? What steps can you take to intentionally cultivate reliance on the Spirit?

Week 6 Group Discussion

1. Galatians 4:4–5 shows us that at just the right time, God sent his son, Jesus Christ, to redeem us from the curse of the law. How does this truth help us trust God's timing and ultimate plan, especially when we are faced with situations that we don't understand or are seemingly impossible to fix? Share practical ways that we can build our trust in God and help others do the same when we may be struggling to trust him.

2. Galatians 4:6 says, "Because you are sons, God has sent the Spirit of his Son into our hearts, crying, 'Abba! Father!'" What does this verse say about our identity as daughters of God and also as people who are sealed with the very Spirit of God? How can we find comfort in knowing that God invites us into a close, intimate relationship with him through his Spirit?

3. How does understanding the gospel as a call to both know God and be known by him affect our relationship with him? Considering the radical transformation that this divine-human encounter brings, is it possible for us to turn back to our old way of life? What practical things can we do to ensure that we do not turn away from God?

4. Sometimes, consciously or unconsciously, we wrongly judge other believers by their observance of religious days. Perhaps we look down on those who don't attend church on Christmas or Easter. Or maybe we view attending church on Sundays as the only indicator of faith. How can we avoid falling into the trap of measuring people's righteousness by what they do as opposed to accepting them on the basis on their faith in Jesus Christ?

5. Have you ever experienced a situation where a false teacher or maybe even a bad leader caused division and alienation in your church or home? What practical steps can we take to recognize and protect ourselves and our church communities from the influence of false teachers?

6. How does Paul's allegory of Hagar and Sarah help us better understand the contrast between the old covenant of the law and the new covenant of grace? Share how the difference between Hagar and Sarah clarifies what it means to live under the promise rather than under the law.

Week 7

FREEDOM IN THE SPIRIT
(GALATIANS 5:1–26)

The fruit of the Spirit is freedom—
freedom to love, to exude joy, to manifest
peace, to display patience, and so on.

TIMOTHY GEORGE

VIDEO 8

Welcoming a new puppy into our family has been the experience of a lifetime. From joy and laughter to frustration and regret, our journey has had many ups and downs. Our puppy, affectionately known as Ken Ken, has quickly become the main attraction in our home. He is the perfect blend of youthful innocence, undeniable mischief, and utter cuteness! Unfortunately, this little guy likes to turn household items (like my prized collection of books) into chew toys. This has forced us to establish a safe play area for him, and we call this area "the puppy pen." It protects him (and our belongings) from harm. But it's no surprise that Ken Ken hates this kind of restriction. When we give him an opportunity to roam freely, he delightfully dashes through the house faster than our eyes can follow.

The truth is, no one likes to be confined and restricted—God made us to be free! And it was this spiritual freedom that Paul called the Galatians to in chapter 5 of his letter. Just as our sweet pup experiences the joy of not being confined to the puppy pen, so were the Galatians called to rejoice in the spiritual freedom that was won for them by Christ. And Paul urges them to fully embrace this freedom. His message is simple but profound: If Christ has set you free, then be free! Don't get tied up in the chains of legalism, especially the belief that one must conform to Jewish religious standards to be a part of God's family.

This week, we will dig into a widely known passage of Scripture—Paul's description of the fruit of the Spirit. In this passage, Paul isn't just giving us a guideline for morality; he's showing us the evidence of true freedom in Christ. The fruit of the Spirit is the outworking of a life led by the Spirit and lived in line with God's will—a life no longer bound by the law but flourishing in the freedom Christ provides.

Key Terms

Circumcision: the practice of removing the foreskin from a male's genitals, which functioned as a sign of God's covenant with his people

The Trinity: the Christian doctrine that identifies God as one who exists in three coequal and coeternal persons—Father, Son (Jesus), and Spirit

Yoke: a harness used to join two animals together for the purpose of work such as plowing fields

WEEK 7 | DAY 1
Galatians 5:1–6

Read Galatians 5. After reading the entire chapter, focus on verses 1–6 and answer the following questions:

- In verse 1, Paul asserts that in Christ, all believers are truly free. What two directives does Paul then give?

- When Paul was writing his letter to the Galatians, they were living under Roman rule and experiencing oppression. In light of this, how would Paul's description of the Galatians' returning to the law for justification as taking on the "yoke of slavery" have resonated with them?

- Paul uses a direct and authoritative tone in verse 2 when he says, "Look: I, Paul, say to you . . ." What does this tone reveal about his concern for the Galatians and his role as an apostle?

- In verse 3, when Paul says, "I testify again to every man who accepts circumcision that he is obligated to keep the whole law," he is making a critical theological and practical point about the nature of commitment to the Mosaic law, which had 613 commandments. According to verse 3, what would a person have to do to be made right with God by keeping the law?

- Paul draws a stark contrast between circumcision and faith in Christ. What does Paul's argument imply about the effectiveness of circumcision compared to faith in Christ for gaining salvation and righteousness?

Galatians 5:1–26

- In verse 4, Paul says, "You are severed from Christ, you who would be justified by the law; you have fallen away from grace." What does this statement say about the consequences of seeking justification through the law?

- Consider the fact that God's kingdom (into which believers are saved) has already been inaugurated by Christ but will not be fully realized or consummated until his second coming. How does Paul's encouragement to "wait for the hope of righteousness" (v. 5) help us understand what it means to live by faith today?

- In what ways does the tension between the present reality of our justification and the future completion of our salvation influence our lives, decisions, and hope as believers?

☐ Read the following passages: Ephesians 6:23, 1 Thessalonians 1:3, and James 2:18–22. In light of these, what does Paul mean when he refers to "faith working through love" in Galatians 5:6? How might believers display such faith?

Personal Reflection

How does recognizing the full scope of our freedom in Christ (Gal. 5:1–6) transform our understanding of grace? How does it shape our approach to spiritual disciplines? How does freedom in Christ influence the decisions you make on a day-to-day basis, especially in areas where you are tempted to earn God's favor?

WEEK 7 | DAY 2
Galatians 5:7–12

Reread Galatians 5. After rereading the entire chapter, focus on verses 7–12 and answer the following questions:

- In verse 7, Paul says, "You were running well. Who hindered you from obeying the truth?" What does this say about the Galatians' initial progress in faith? How would Paul's question have prompted the Galatians to examine the influences that they had allowed to shape their spiritual lives?

- In verse 8, Paul asserts that claims like "Circumcision is a means of justification" do not come from God, the one who calls believers. If these beliefs do not come from God, who do they come from? How does recognizing the source of teachings help us practice discernment?

- Paul uses the metaphor of leaven (yeast) in baking to illustrate how even a small deviation from gospel truth can affect an entire community. How does this image help us understand the impact of allowing minor errors or false teachings into our churches?

- What does Paul's confidence that the Galatians will hold firm to the true gospel (and "take no other view"; v. 10) reveal about the nature of Christian assurance and hope?

- Paul says in verse 11 that he was being persecuted for preaching the true gospel of salvation through the cross of Christ rather than acts like circumcision. Why does Paul suggest that if he preached circumcision, the "offense of the cross" would be removed? What do Paul's words in this verse reveal about the radical nature of the gospel message? Take a moment to write out a few reasons why Paul's teachings faced such strong resistance from the Judaizers.

Galatians 5:1–26

◘ Note the intensity of Paul's wish in verse 12 for those who "unsettle" the Galatians to "emasculate" themselves. Paul's language here is intentionally harsh. What does it reveal about the seriousness with which he views distorting the gospel?

Personal Reflection

How can you apply Paul's exhortation to remain true to the gospel in your own life, especially when faced with conflicting teachings? How can the principles in this passage help us guard ourselves and our churches from false teaching?

WEEK 7 | DAY 3
Galatians 5:13–15

Reread Galatians 5. After rereading the entire chapter, focus on verses 13–15 and answer the following questions:

- In verse 13, Paul says the Galatians were "called to freedom." How does this Christian freedom differ from worldly concepts of freedom?

- Paul warns us to not use our freedom as an opportunity for the flesh. What might this look like practically? How can we ensure that our freedom is used rightly?

- How is serving one another through love a manifestation of Christian freedom? How does this principle challenge the modern understanding of freedom as serving oneself?

Galatians 5:1–26

- Consider Paul's statement in verse 14 that the whole law is fulfilled in the command to love your neighbor as yourself. How does this simplify your understanding of what God requires from us?

- In what ways can you practice loving your neighbor in daily life? How does this command shape your interactions and priorities?

- Note Paul's warning in verse 15 against biting and devouring one another. Here, Paul is using figurative language to describe an aggressive way of relating to others. In what ways can this show up in our interactions with others? What are the potential consequences of such behavior for our relationships with other believers?

◻ How can believers guard against the tendency toward the kind of conflict and division mentioned in verse 15? What role do mutual love and respect play in this?

Personal Reflection

Sometimes serving in love means doing the very thing that makes you a little uncomfortable. It might require giving up your preferred way of doing something or supporting someone else's idea instead of your own. In what ways have you been led to serve fellow believers in love? How can you intentionally practice serving in love (and doing so with joy) even when it might be a bit uncomfortable?

Galatians 5:1–26 147

WEEK 7 | DAY 4
Galatians 5:16–21

Reread Galatians 5. After rereading the entire chapter, focus on verses 16–21 and answer the following questions:

◘ According to verse 16, what does it mean to "walk by the Spirit"?

◘ In verse 17, Paul says the desires of the flesh are against the Spirit. Can you think of times in your own life when you've felt this conflict?

◘ According to verse 18, what does being led by the Spirit set us free from?

◘ List the works of the flesh. Why is it important to recognize the works (i.e., behaviors) of the flesh? How can believers actively avoid practicing the works of the flesh?

◘ In verse 21, Paul warns that those who engage in works of the flesh will not inherit the kingdom of God. How does this warning influence your choices and actions?

Personal Reflection

In what ways have you been tempted by the works of the flesh? Where do you need to grow in demonstrating the fruit of the Spirit? Write out a prayer asking for God's help in those areas.

WEEK 7 | DAY 5

Galatians 5:22–26

Reread Galatians 5. After rereading the entire chapter, focus on verses 22–26 and answer the following questions:

◘ List the aspects of the fruit of the Spirit. How do these reflect the character of the Holy Spirit?

◘ How does the fruit of the Spirit contrast with the works of the flesh mentioned in Galatians 5:19–21? Why is it important for Christians to understand this distinction when seeking to live a life that reflects Christ?

- Why does Paul say there is no law against such things as the fruit of the Spirit?

- How can a Christian "live by the Spirit" and "keep in step with the Spirit" (v. 25)? What might these look like in practical terms?

- What does it mean to crucify "the flesh with its passions and desires" (v. 24)?

- Why does Paul warn against attitudes such as conceit, provocation, and envy in the context of discussing the fruit of the Spirit? How do these warnings help us understand the importance of humility and unity within a Christian community?

Galatians 5:1–26   151

🔸 Reflect on each aspect of the fruit of the Spirit. Which aspects are flourishing in your life? Which aspects are languishing?

🔸 How can understanding and developing the fruit of the Spirit affect your relationships with people in your community and church?

Did You Know?

When the apostle Paul encourages the Galatians to "keep in step with the Spirit," he is using the military concept of falling in line. Simply put, believers should aim for conformity to Christ as soldiers under the leadership of the Spirit. Theologian Timothy George explains this more plainly, saying, "Just as we put to death the old existence of the flesh in mortification, so too we move forward in the life of faith by keeping in step with the Spirit in our attitudes, conduct, and lifestyle."[1]

◘ What are some practical steps you can take to cultivate the fruit of the Spirit in your daily life?

Personal Reflection

As you reflect on the fruit of the Spirit, remember that it is a collective byproduct of the Spirit's work, not a list of individual traits to pick and choose from. How can you guard against focusing on one aspect, such as love, while neglecting others, such as self-control? And how can you stay eager to walk in step with the Spirit without slipping into a works-based mentality?

Week 7 Group Discussion

1. Imagine soldiers standing firm on the battlefield while the general fights on their behalf. That is what Christ does for believers. With this image in mind, think about how Paul's command to "stand firm" in Galatians 5:1 provides practical insight for maintaining our freedom in Christ. How can we encourage one another to stand firm, especially when facing trials and temptations?

2. In Galatians 5:3–6, Paul makes the point that to truly be justified by the law, one would have to keep every part of it perfectly at all times, which is impossible. Thus, keeping just one law, such as circumcision, actually counts for nothing. What really matters is "faith working through love." How does this truth help you understand what it means to live by faith? How can we practically demonstrate our faith not by works of the law but by showing love?

3. How does Paul's instruction in verse 9 help us understand the seriousness of false teaching and the potential impact it can have on our churches and other neighboring churches? What responsibility do believers have to reject and expose perversions of the gospel? What are some possible side effects that might arise if false teaching is left unchecked in our churches and other Christian communities?

4. How can believers use their freedom to serve one another in love? Share examples of how you can intentionally serve those in the family of faith as well as those who have rejected the gospel.

5. How does Paul's focus on the command to "love your neighbor as yourself" (5:14) shape our understanding of what it means to truly live as a Christian? How are you loving your neighbor as yourself in concrete ways?

6. In verse 14, Paul highlights the role of the law and shows us that it was given to guide us toward loving God and people well. How does understanding the ultimate purpose of the law help us view it as something that is good and useful?

7. Paul concludes Galatians 5 by contrasting the works of the flesh with the fruit of the Spirit. How do the works of the flesh hinder the flourishing of our Christian communities and damage our relationships? How does living by the Spirit build up our communities and transform them? If you feel led, share with the group how you've seen the damage caused by the works of the flesh and the blessings of the fruit of the Spirit.

Week 8

LIVING FREE IN CHRIST
(GALATIANS 6:1–18)

Human friendship, in which we bear one another's burdens, is part of the purpose of God for His people. So we should not keep our burdens to ourselves, but rather seek a Christian friend who will help to bear them with us.

JOHN STOTT

VIDEO 9

Remember when I shared, back in week 4 of our study, about my family's home-buying adventures? Well, that experience led us to another one—gardening! After we purchased our home, there was a lot of work that needed to be done. The biggest eyesores were the front lawn and flower beds. In all honesty, we had to ignore this mess of a yard to even see the potential of living in the home at all.

So fixing our lawn was the first order of business after the purchase was finalized. One Saturday morning, I woke up early to get started on pulling up all the old, wilted flowers and bushes and cleaning out the timeworn mulch. While working, I noticed that one of the plants to my far left looked a bit different. As I moved closer, I realized that it was actually a tomato plant. My initial thought was, How in the world did tomatoes end up in the flower beds? The answer was obvious: Tomato seeds somehow had been planted there!

While my thumb isn't as green as I'd like it to be, I do know the basic concepts of gardening—you will reap whatever you sow. If basil is planted, then basil will spring up. If roses are planted, then roses will appear. And if tomatoes are planted, then—you guessed it—tomatoes will arise. This simple principle of reaping what you sow is at the center of Galatians 6. Here, Paul guides us through the cause and effect of our spiritual lives. If we invest our time, energy, and resources into pursuing selfish desires, then we will inevitably harvest death and decay. But if we pursue a life of godliness that honors God, then we will reap a spiritual harvest that leads to flourishing and eternal life.

Key Terms

Transgression: the breaking of God's law

New creation: the transformation and renewal of life that occurs when a person is united with Christ by the Holy Spirit, which also signifies the believer's new identity and purpose and points to the ultimate restoration of all creation that will occur when Jesus Christ returns

Reaping: the gathering of a harvest in farming or gardening, often used in the Bible as a metaphor for living with the consequences of our actions, whether good or bad

Galatians 6:1–18

As we wrap up our study with the last chapter of Galatians, let us consider the areas of our lives where we may be sowing the wrong seeds. Are you harboring bitterness or always finding yourself at the center of conflicts and quarreling? Are you pursuing your own selfish way of life while ignoring God's call to serve others in love? This week, I hope you are encouraged to be diligent spiritual gardeners who plant good, God-glorifying seeds that grow into a bountiful spiritual blessing. Let's finish strong!

WEEK 8 | DAY 1
Galatians 6:1–3

Read Galatians 6. After reading the entire chapter, focus on verses 1–3 and answer the following questions:

- In verse 1, Paul encourages the Galatians to restore transgressors "in a spirit of gentleness." Read 1 Corinthians 4:21 and 2 Timothy 2:25. How do these passages shed light on what it means to restore someone in this way?

- What are practical ways we can restore someone gently in the church?

◻ In the latter half of verse 1, Paul advises the Galatians to gently restore a fellow believer who has fallen into sin. How does adopting this approach affect the way believers develop healthy, biblical relationships with one another? Why is it important to remain aware of our own vulnerability to temptation as we do so?

◻ In verse 2, Paul speaks of bearing one another's burdens. The Greek word used here means "to cause to come to a higher position, pick up, [or] take up."[1] Practically speaking, what does it look like to bear one another's burdens? How have you experienced this in your church?

◻ Read John 13:34 and 1 John 4:21. How do these passages shape your understanding of fulfilling the law of Christ by bearing one another's burdens?

Galatians 6:1–18

▢ In verse 3, Paul warns against thinking too highly of oneself. Why is humility a necessary virtue of the Christian life, and how can a lack of humility lead to self-deception and misunderstanding of our true spiritual state?

Personal Reflection

Has there ever been a time in your life when you've overestimated your own importance or abilities? How has this attitude affected your relationships? What, if anything, led you to realize your egotism?

WEEK 8 | DAY 2
Galatians 6:4–5

Reread Galatians 6. After rereading the entire chapter, focus on verses 4–5 and answer the following questions:

- In verse 4, Paul encourages each of the Galatians to "test his own work." Read 2 Corinthians 13:5 and consider what it means to test your own work. How can self-examination positively affect your spiritual growth and your relationships with other believers?

- According to verse 4, why does Paul say we should test our own work?

- Do Paul's words in this passage resonate with you in any way? How can we apply this verse to our lives when we are tempted to compare ourselves with others?

Galatians 6:1–18

- Read Romans 14:10–12. How does this passage relate to Paul's encouragement in Galatians 6:5 to "bear [your] own load"? How does the principle of personal responsibility relate to the earlier verses (vv. 2–3) about bearing one another's burdens?

- What does it mean to bear one's own load in the church?

- How does taking responsibility for one's own actions demonstrate spiritual growth and maturity?

Personal Reflection

Take a moment to reflect on your own life over the past year. Are you more loving or less loving than you were at this time last year? How would you measure your gentleness or self-control today compared to six months ago? Reflecting on these questions can help you assess your spiritual health. As you consider these things, take time to pause and pray, asking God for help in areas of weakness.

WEEK 8 | DAY 3
Galatians 6:6–8

Reread Galatians 6. After rereading the entire chapter, focus on verses 6–8 and answer the following questions:

- In verse 6, what does Paul encourage those who are taught the Bible to do? How can this be applied in modern contexts, particularly to how we value and support spiritual leaders?

- Why does Paul warn against deception and mocking of God (v. 7)? Why do you think Paul emphasizes this point? List some ways one could become deceived or mock God.

◘ In what areas of your spiritual life do you need to be more vigilant to avoid deception or complacency?

....

....

....

◘ Consider the fact that "whatever one sows, that will he also reap" (v. 7). What does this suggest about cause and effect in one's spiritual life? What biblical or real-life examples can you think of that illustrate this principle?

....

....

....

◘ What specific behaviors or attitudes might reflect sowing to the flesh versus sowing to the Spirit (v. 8)? Write them in the table below.

Sowing to the Flesh	Sowing to the Spirit

Galatians 6:1–18

◘ Think about the broader implications of reaping corruption (the effect of sowing to the flesh) and reaping eternal life (the effect of sowing to the Spirit):

- Does corruption refer only to physical decay and moral disgrace, or could it also imply a breakdown in relationships, community, and personal well-being?

- Is eternal life just about life after death, or does it also include a quality of life here and now? How might sowing to the flesh affect one's peace, joy, and fulfillment in the Spirit?

- How can understanding the difference between living for temporary, worldly rewards (corruption) and living with a view toward eternal life shape our daily choices and priorities?

Personal Reflection

Are there any areas of your life where you might be sowing to the flesh instead of sowing to the Spirit? Consider both the actions and attitudes that are associated with these two behaviors. What are the immediate and long-term effects of these choices in your personal life, relationships, and overall spiritual health?

WEEK 8 | DAY 4
Galatians 6:9–10

Reread Galatians 6. After rereading the entire chapter, focus on verses 9–10 and answer the following questions:

- List specific actions or behaviors that might be considered "doing good" (v. 9). Are there examples that you can think of from other parts of Scripture that illuminate what this entails? (Hint: Read 1 Cor. 15:58; 2 Thess. 3:13; 1 Tim. 6:18.)

- What challenges or factors might lead to weariness in doing good? How does Paul address these? (Hint: Pay attention to Paul's words and tone in the latter part of v. 9.)

- In verse 9, Paul says, "In due season we will reap, if we do not give up." What kind of harvest is Paul referring to in this context? How does this idea of reaping encourage perseverance in doing good?

- In verse 10, Paul advises the Galatians to do good "as [they] have opportunity." What does an opportunity to do good look like? How can you identify such opportunities in your daily life?

- Read Ephesians 2:19, 1 Timothy 5:8, and Hebrews 3:6. Why might Paul emphasize doing good "especially to those who are of the household of faith" (v. 10)?

- Think about the connection between faith, action, and service. How does your faith motivate and shape your actions when serving others?

Galatians 6:1–18

Personal Reflection

Over the past months or years, in what ways have you done good to others? In what ways have you failed to do good to others? In what ways can you improve in doing good to others?

WEEK 8 | DAY 5
Galatians 6:11–18

Reread Galatians 6. After rereading the entire chapter, focus on verses 11–18 and answer the following questions:

◻ In verse 11, Paul mentions that he writes with "large letters," which may indicate that instead of using a scribe as he often did because of his limited eyesight, he took up the pen himself. Why do you think Paul would make a point to let the Galatians know it was really him writing? How might this personal touch reinforce his message to them?

◻ What motivations does Paul attribute to those advocating for circumcision (vv. 12–13)? What do these motivations suggest about their understanding and practice of faith?

Galatians 6:1–18

- In light of verses 13–14, what should be our only basis for boasting?

- What does Paul mean when he says, "Neither circumcision counts for anything, nor uncircumcision, but a new creation" (v. 15)? How do Paul's words here help us understand our true identity in Christ? Specifically, how should the Galatians (and all followers of Christ) see themselves in light of this new identity?

- Starting in verse 16, Paul gives a conditional benediction to the Galatians. How does this differ from the benedictions Paul gives to the Philippians (4:21–23) and Ephesians (6:21–24)? What are the conditions of Paul's benediction to the Galatians, and why do you think he made his benediction conditional? (Note: It might be helpful to read this verse and the preceding verse in the CSB or NLT.)

- In verse 17, Paul mentions that he bears the marks—possibly meaning physical scars—of Jesus on his body. What does this say about Paul's life and ministry? How do these marks serve as evidence of his dedication to preaching the gospel and enduring hardships for Christ?

- Paul concludes his letter to the Galatians by saying, "The grace of our Lord Jesus Christ be with your spirit, brothers. Amen" (v. 18). How does this summarize the overarching message of Galatians?

Personal Reflection

How have Paul's teachings about grace in his letter to the Galatians influenced your understanding of what it means to be saved? How has studying Galatians helped you be a better disciple and evangelist?

Week 8 Group Discussion

1. At the beginning of Galatians 6, Paul provides instruction on exact ways we can live together in Christian community. What does Paul's use of the word "brothers" say about how the local church functions?

2. What are some specific ways that you can bear the burdens of fellow believers in your church?

3. Recall a time when you were gently corrected. How did you respond? What was the overall impact of this gentle correction? How can we be more intentional in offering correction to fellow believers while heeding Paul's encouragement to do so gently?

4. How do Paul's words "Do not be deceived: God is not mocked" remind us that nothing ever falls through the cracks in God's economy (6:7)? How does this truth motivate us to live honorably before God and in reverential fear of him?

5. Consider the principle "Whatever one sows, that will he also reap" (v. 7). How have you experienced this in your own life? Have you reaped the bad fruit that comes from sowing to the flesh? What about the good fruit that comes with sowing to the Spirit?

6. Have you ever felt so tired, drained, or spent that you simply wanted to give up on doing things God's way? How does Paul's encouragement in verse 9 to not grow weary of doing good bring you hope? How do Paul's words build your enthusiasm to keep going even when life gets tough?

7. Think about what it means to be a new creation in Christ who is not primarily defined by ethnicity, gender, cultural traditions, or good works. How does understanding this help us walk in the freedom of Christ?

8. What has been the most insightful or life-changing truth that you've studied in Galatians? Share with the group and take time to pray, thanking God for the blessing of his holy word.

Galatians Wrap-Up

Congratulations! You just finished studying Galatians. What a way to show your dedication and desire to grow deeper in God's word. Take a moment to praise God for the blessing of intentional and consistent time studying the Bible. Rest assured, you will reap an eternal reward. Also, if you went through this book with other sisters in Christ, take time to thank God for that sweet fellowship. I hope that studying with others has brought you into a greater appreciation for Christian community and a deeper relationship with your spiritual family.

Even if your journey through this study was a little rocky or you feel as if you may have missed a few things, that's okay! The beauty of having God's word written down for us is that we get to read it over and over. In the days, weeks, months, and years ahead, I encourage you to regularly put your life under the microscope of Scripture. What spiritual disciplines can you practice regularly to help you integrate God's truth more deeply into your daily walk with Christ? How can you continue to grow in your understanding and application of the gospel? How can you and your church family continue living out the message of Galatians? Whether it's implementing certain practices to guard against and combat false teaching or cultivating an environment of diverse fellowship, there are so many ways your local church can collectively demonstrate the teachings found in Galatians. It's through our public witness, both individually and communally, that the world truly sees the transformative power of the gospel.

If you are excited and motivated to continue studying the book of Galatians, there are tons of resources available to deepen your understanding of this letter in particular and, more broadly, Pauline theology. Many accessible commentaries, books, and digital tools are available to supplement your studies. Below is a curated list of resources on Galatians that you might find useful, many of which I used while developing this study.

Commentaries on Galatians

George, Timothy. *Galatians*. The New American Commentary, vol. 30. Holman, 2020.

McKnight, Scot. *Galatians*. The NIV Application Commentary. Zondervan, 1995.

Moo, Douglas J. *Galatians*. Baker Exegetical Commentary on the New Testament. Baker, 2013.

Ryken, Philip Graham. *Galatians*. Reformed Expository Commentary. P&R, 2005.

Stott, John. *The Message of Galatians: Only One Way*. The Bible Speaks Today. InterVarsity Press, 2020.

Monographs on Galatians

Keller, Tim. *Galatians for You*. Good Book Company, 2013.

Platt, David, and Tony Merida. *Exalting Jesus in Galatians*. Holman Reference, 2014.

Digital Study Tools

Ligonier Ministries (articles), https://www.ligonier.org/
Logos Bible Software (Bible study software), https://www.logos.com
Monergism (articles), https://www.monergism.com
The English Standard Version (Bible), https://www.esv.org

An Encouragement

Finally, I'd like to leave you with words of encouragement and a blessing. Remember that your identity is found in the grace of God. You are loved, you are called, and you are empowered to live out the truth of the gospel with courage, conviction, and compassion. Let the teachings of Paul to the Galatians always remind you of the freedom you have in Christ and the responsibility you carry to live as a woman of the cross.

I challenge you to take practical steps in response to your study of Galatians, whether in spiritual disciplines, involvement in your church, or more broadly through service in your community. Don't allow the things that you've learned to slip away. Make every effort to continue growing in grace and in the knowledge of God (2 Pet. 3:18). Be intentional about your witness as a believer to a lost and dying world. In fact, if you haven't already, take a few minutes right now to write down something you can do in response to this Bible study.

Finally, I invite you to use the prayer prompts found in the appendix of this book to pray through the truths in Galatians. I hope you can use these prompts to cultivate a more intentional and consistent prayer life that is centered on the word of God.

Go forth in grace and peace, living as a testimony to the transformative power of the gospel. May God richly bless you now and forevermore.

Appendix

PRAYING THROUGH GALATIANS

1. Heavenly Father, I humbly ask you to open up my heart and mind and grant me the wisdom to grasp the depths of your truths and apply them to my life. Illuminate the pages of your word so that I might see your grace and love afresh.

2. Lord, in a world filled with many voices and teachings, strengthen my ability to cling to the truth of the gospel of Jesus Christ. Protect me from deception and empower me to live in the truth of your salvation with firm faith.

3. Almighty God, guide me in seeking your approval above all else. Help me to embrace the gospel not as mere human words, but as your divine truth that transforms my life and orders my steps according to your will.

4. Father, teach me to collaborate with fellow believers, focusing on the shared mission of the gospel for the sake of your kingdom. Help me use my hands and my mind to build up the church and not tear it down.

5. Jesus, deepen my understanding and appreciation of being justified by faith alone. Let this truth liberate me from the chains of self-reliance and lead me into the freedom and rest found in your grace.

6. Holy Spirit, help me to always be sensitive to your presence in my life. Strengthen my faith and open my heart to the fullness of your work and guidance.

7. Merciful Father, thank you for the incredible blessing of being counted among Abraham's children as righteous through faith. Help me to walk in that faith and fully embrace the promises you have extended to those you call your children.

8. Jesus, my Redeemer, thank you for releasing me from the curse of the law and ushering me into the freedom of your grace. Teach me to live and walk daily in that liberty. Help me to never return to a life bound by legalism.

9. Father, open my eyes to see and appreciate the beautiful relationship between your law and your promise fulfilled in Christ. Help me to always anchor my faith in your promises regardless of what is happening in the world around me or in my personal circumstances.

10. Lord, help me see how the law reveals my need for a Savior. In moments when I am reminded of my inability to keep the law, point me toward resting in the work of Christ by faith.

11. Thank you, Father, for making me your precious daughter. Help me to embrace this identity every day. Help me to walk intentionally in the identity that you've given not only to me but also to everyone who comes to you by faith.

12. Abba Father, draw me into a closer relationship with you. May I never stop depending on your Spirit. Keep me tethered to you all the days of my life.

13. Lord, help me to consider not only my own spiritual health but also the spiritual well-being of my brothers and sisters in Christ. Guide me in encouraging and edifying others in their faith. Help me to do so with sincere love and dedication, just as Paul did for the Galatians.

14. Heavenly Father, help me never forget that you are a God who keeps every promise. Help me to fully take hold of the freedom found in the new covenant through Jesus Christ and to live as a child of the promise.

15. Jesus, you have called me to freedom. Help me to stand firm in this freedom and not be burdened again by a yoke of slavery. Teach me to

use my freedom to serve others in love, thereby reflecting your sacrificial love in my actions.

16. Holy Spirit, I desire to walk in step with you and live a life that reflects the fruit of your presence. Help me to discern and resist the desires of the flesh and to consistently live out the fruit of love, joy, peace, patience, kindness, goodness, faithfulness, gentleness, and self-control.

17. O Lord, give me a holy desire to bear the burdens of others and live according to the law of Christ. Show me how I can support those around me in their struggles by carrying their burdens as if they were my own.

18. Father God, remind me of the everlasting blessedness of sowing to please the Spirit rather than the flesh. Give me the wisdom and perseverance to invest in what is eternal and to reap a harvest of righteousness for your glory.

19. Lord Jesus, in a world that often values achievement and status, help me to boast only in you. May I never covet an ounce of your glory. May the whole of my identity be found in you.

20. Lord, thank you for the truths I uncovered and the lessons I learned through studying Galatians. Help me carry this biblical wisdom as I follow you, and help me share these truths with others I encounter.

21. Heavenly Father, let your grace be the foundation for my beliefs, actions, and responses to others. Help me to give grace to others just as freely as it has been given to me.

22. Gracious God, teach me that self-reliance means nothing in your economy. Help me to rest in your grace and find it sufficient for all circumstances, especially times of struggle and weakness.

23. Jesus, you have called me to a glorious freedom. Help me to live in this freedom wisely and lovingly. Help me to use my freedom not for selfish gain but as an opportunity to serve others in your name.

24. Holy Spirit, cultivate in me the fruit of your presence. May love, joy, peace, patience, kindness, goodness, faithfulness, gentleness, and self-control be evident in my life, not separately but collectively. Help me to follow your leading in every aspect of my life.

25. Lord God, give me the strength and compassion needed to bear the burdens of others. Teach me to offer support and encouragement in a way that honors you. Show me how I can lighten the load of a sister in need. Let me not be blind to the struggles of those around me. Give me an awareness to see and wisdom to help.

26. Heavenly Father, guide me to walk in the Spirit each day. In moments when I am unsure of what to do, help me recognize and follow the Spirit's leading with firm faith and full assurance that you are sovereign over all.

27. Everlasting God, remind me every day that whatever I sow, I will also reap. If I sow to the flesh, I will reap destruction. But if I sow to the Spirit, I will reap life. Help me to always sow seeds that honor and bring you glory.

28. Jesus, strengthen the bonds within our church community. Help us to live out the teachings found in Galatians. Help us to be consistent in showing love, carrying burdens, and working for the good of all, especially those in the family of faith.

29. Lord Jesus, keep my eyes fixed on you. You are my strength. Your love and sacrifice are matchless. Let all my boasting be found in you. May the words of my mouth always declare your goodness and glory, now and forever.

30. Heavenly Father, grant me the grace to live completely as your child. Help me to remember that your promises were good for the saints of old and are also good for me right now in this moment. Remind me that whatever my need is, you have already provided.

Notes

Introduction
1. See *Merriam-Webster*, https://www.merriam-webster.com/.

Week 1, Day 2: Galatians 1:6–10
1. *ESV Study Bible* (Crossway, 2007), 2241–43.

Week 2, Day 3: Galatians 2:11–14
1. Walter Bauer, *A Greek-English Lexicon of the New Testament and Other Early Christian Literature*, 3rd ed., rev. and ed. Frederick W. Danker (University of Chicago Press, 2000), 1038.
2. Timothy George, *Galatians*, vol. 30, *The New American Commentary* (Nashville: B&H Publishers, 1994), 170–77.
3. James F. Strange, "Antioch," in *Holman Illustrated Bible Dictionary*, ed. Chad Brand et al. (Nashville, TN: Holman, 2003), 75.

Week 3, Day 1: Galatians 3:1–3
1. Bauer, *Greek-English Lexicon*, 171.

Week 3, Day 5: Galatians 3:13–14
1. Wayne Grudem, *Systematic Theology: An Introduction to Biblical Doctrine*, 2nd ed. (Zondervan, 2020), 1527.

Week 4, Day 5: Galatians 3:23–24
1. This quotation is from the author's personal experience.

Week 5, Day 1: Galatians 3:25
1. Bauer, *Greek-English Lexicon*, 748.

Week 6, Day 1: Galatians 4:1–7
1. George, *Galatians*, 294.

Week 7, Day 5: Galatians 5:22–26
1. George, *Galatians*, 406.

Week 8, Day 1: Galatians 6:1–3
1. Bauer, *Greek-English Lexicon*, 171.